THE GOSPEL of JUDAS

CODEX TCHACOS in 2001

THE GOSPEL
OF JUDAS

from Codex Tchacos

EDITED BY

RODOLPHE KASSER,
MARVIN MEYER,
and GREGOR WURST

NATIONAL GEOGRAPHIC
Washington, D.C.

Published by the National Geographic Society
1145 17th Street, N.W., Washington, D.C. 20036-4688

Copyright © 2006 National Geographic Society

Library of Congress Cataloging-in-Publication Data available on request.

DEFINING TIME PERIODS
Many scholars and editors working today in the multicultural discipline of world history use terminology that does not impose the standards of one culture on others. As recommended by the scholars who have contributed to the National Geographic Society's publication of the Gospel of Judas, this book uses the terms BCE (before the Common Era) and CE (Common Era). BCE refers to the same time period as B.C. (before Christ), and CE refers to the same time period as A.D. (anno Domini, a Latin phrase meaning "in the year of the Lord").

ISBN-10: 1-4262-0042-0
ISBN-13: 978-1-4262-0042-7

One of the world's largest nonprofit scientific and educational organizations, the National Geographic Society was founded in 1888 "for the increase and diffusion of geographic knowledge." Fulfilling this mission, the Society educates and inspires millions every day through its magazines, books, television programs, videos, maps and atlases, research grants, the National Geographic Bee, teacher workshops, and innovative classroom materials. The Society is supported through membership dues, charitable gifts, and income from the sale of its educational products. This support is vital to National Geographic's mission to increase global understanding and promote conservation of our planet through exploration, research, and education.

For more information, please call 1-800-NGS LINE (647-5463), write to the Society at the above address, or visit the Society's Web site at www.nationalgeographic.com.

Interior design by Melissa Farris

CONTENTS

The concluding page of the Gospel of Judas

INTRODUCTION

Over the years the sands of Egypt have surrendered countless treasures and archaeological wonders, and now they have yielded another spectacular find: the Gospel of Judas, recently discovered and published here for the first time.

The very title of the text, the Gospel of Judas—Judas Iscariot—is shocking. In the New Testament gospels and most of the Christian tradition, Judas Iscariot is portrayed as the quintessential traitor, the betrayer of Jesus who turns his master in to the Roman authorities, and there is little in his character that could connect him with the gospel, or "good news," of Jesus. In the Gospel of Luke it is said that Satan enters into Judas and drives him to his despicable deed, and in the Gospel of John, Jesus addresses the twelve disciples and says that one of them, Judas, is a devil. The end of Judas, according to the New Testament, is as ignominious as his actions. He takes blood money from the authorities for his betrayal of Jesus, and either he hangs himself (as in Matthew) or his belly is ripped open and he dies in a ghastly fashion (as in Acts). In Christian art, Judas typically is shown doing what has earned him a place in infamy, betraying Jesus with a kiss—the Judas kiss.

Yet even in the New Testament, there is something captivating about Judas Iscariot. The account of Judas betraying Jesus remains a story of great power and poignancy: Jesus is betrayed by one of his closest friends. In the New Testament gospels, Judas is part of the inner circle of disciples of Jesus, and according to the Gospel of John, Judas functions as the treasurer of the group and is entrusted with whatever funds Jesus and the disciples might have had. Further, at the Last Supper, didn't Jesus himself tell Judas to do what he had to do, and say to do it quickly? Wasn't all this part of the divine plan—that Jesus should die for the sins of people and rise from the dead on the third day? Without Judas and his kiss, would the Crucifixion and Resurrection ever have taken place?

The enigma of Judas Iscariot, the disciple and betrayer of Jesus, has been explored by many who have wondered about Judas's character and motivation. The literature on Judas is rich and includes well-known works of academic scholarship and modern literature—Jorge Luis Borges's *Three Versions of Judas,* Mikhail Bulgakov's *The Master and Margarita,* Hans-Josef Klauck's *Judas: Ein Jünger des Herrn,* William Klassen's *Judas: Betrayer or Friend of Jesus?,* Hyam Maccoby's *Judas Iscariot and the Myth of Jewish Evil,* and Marcel Pagnol's play, *Judas.* In the rock musical *Jesus Christ Superstar,* Judas Iscariot nearly steals the show, and his presence and music provide a more sympathetic view of the depth of his devotion to Jesus. In the song "With God on Our Side," Bob Dylan sings of Judas:

You'll have to decide
Whether Judas Iscariot
Had God on his side.

The Judas Iscariot of the Gospel of Judas is the betrayer of Jesus, but he is simultaneously the hero of the gospel. He says to Jesus, "I know who you are and where you have come from. You are from the immortal realm of Barbelo. And I am not worthy to utter the name of the one who has sent you." In the spiritual world of the Gospel of Judas, to confess that Jesus is from "the immortal realm of Barbelo" is to confess that he is a divine being, and to declare the ineffability of the name of the one who sent Jesus is to profess that the true God is the infinite Spirit of the universe. Unlike the other disciples, who misunderstand Jesus and cannot bear to stand before his face, Judas understands who Jesus is, takes his place before him, and learns from him.

Judas finally betrays Jesus in the Gospel of Judas, but he does so knowingly, and at the sincere request of Jesus. Jesus says to Judas, with reference to the other disciples, "You will exceed all of them. For you will sacrifice the man that clothes me." According to the Gospel of Judas, Jesus is a savior not because of the mortal flesh that he wears but because he can reveal the soul or spiritual person who is within, and the true home of Jesus is not this imperfect world below but the divine world of light and life. For Jesus in the Gospel of Judas, death is no tragedy, nor is it a necessary evil to bring about the forgiveness of sins. In the Gospel of Judas, unlike the New Testament gospels, Jesus laughs a great deal. He laughs at the foibles of the disciples and the absurdities in human life. Death, as the exit from this absurd physical existence, is not to be feared or dreaded. Far from being an occasion of sadness, death is the means by which Jesus is liberated from the flesh in order that he might return to his heavenly home, and by betraying Jesus, Judas helps his friend discard his body and free his inner self, the divine self.

This perspective of the Gospel of Judas is different in a number of respects from that of the New Testament gospels. During the formative period of the Christian Church, numerous gospels were composed in addition to the New Testament gospels of Matthew, Mark, Luke, and John. Among the other gospels that have survived, as a whole or in part, are the Gospel of Truth and the Gospels of Thomas, Peter, Philip, Mary, the Ebionites, the Nazoreans, the Hebrews, and the Egyptians, to name a few, and these gospels demonstrate the rich diversity of perspectives within early Christianity. The Gospel of Judas was yet another of the gospels written by early Christians as they attempted to articulate, in one way or another, who Jesus is and how one should follow him.

The Gospel of Judas may be classified as what is often called a gnostic gospel. Probably composed around the middle of the second century, most likely on the basis of earlier ideas and sources, the Gospel of Judas represents an early form of spirituality that emphasizes *gnōsis*, or "knowledge"—mystical knowledge, knowledge of God and the essential oneness of the self with God. This spirituality is commonly described as "gnostic," but there was a debate in the ancient world over the use of the term, and that debate continues to the present day among scholars. Such a direct approach to God as is to be found in gnostic spirituality requires no intermediary—after all, God is the spirit and light within—and the evidence from the early Church and the heresiologists (heresy hunters) within the Church indicates that the priests and bishops were not pleased with these free-thinking gnostics. The writings of the heresiologists are filled with accusations that gnostics entertained evil thoughts and engaged in illicit activities. Polemics is not a pretty business, and documents with polemical intentions, such as those of the heresiologists, frequently try to discredit their opponents by raising suspicions about their thought and life. The gnostic Gospel of Judas returns the favor by accusing the leaders and members of the emerging orthodox Church of all sorts of unsavory behavior. According to the Gospel of Judas, these rival Christians are simply lackeys of the God who rules this world below, and their lives reflect his disgusting ways.

The Gospel of Judas makes mention of Seth, well known from the biblical book of Genesis, and concludes that human beings with the knowledge of God belong to the generation of Seth. This particular form of gnostic thought is often described by scholars as Sethian. In the story told in the Book of Genesis, Seth, third son of

Adam and Eve, was born after the tragic violence in the dysfunctional first family, which left Abel dead and Cain banished. Seth, it is suggested, represents a new beginning for humanity. To belong to the generation of Seth, then, according to the Gospel of Judas and similar Sethian books, is to be part of enlightened humanity. That is the good news of salvation in Sethian texts like the Gospel of Judas.

In the central part of this gospel, Jesus teaches Judas the mysteries of the universe. In the Gospel of Judas, as in other gnostic gospels, Jesus is primarily a teacher and revealer of wisdom and knowledge, not a savior who dies for the sins of the world. For gnostics, the fundamental problem in human life is not sin but ignorance, and the best way to address this problem is not through faith but through knowledge. In the Gospel of Judas, Jesus imparts to Judas—and to the readers of the gospel—the knowledge that can eradicate ignorance and lead to an awareness of oneself and God.

This revelatory section of the Gospel of Judas, however, may present challenges to modern readers. The challenges arise chiefly because the point of view of the Sethian gnostic revelation differs substantially from the philosophy, theology, and cosmology that we have inherited within the Euro-American tradition. Rome and orthodox Christianity eventually won the day, and as Borges once noted concerning the gnostic accounts he was discussing, "Had Alexandria triumphed and not Rome, the extravagant and muddled stories that I have summarized here would be coherent, majestic, and perfectly ordinary." The gnostics of Alexandria and Egypt did not triumph, nor did the Gospel of Judas, in the theological wars that raged during the second, third, and fourth centuries, and consequently texts like the Gospel of Judas, with their different perspectives, contain ideas that sound unusual today.

Nonetheless, the revelation that Jesus imparts to Judas in the Gospel of Judas illustrates a theology and cosmology that are still quite sophisticated. The revelation itself contains few Christian elements, and, if scholars are correct in their understanding of the development of gnostic traditions, the roots of these ideas may go back to the first century or even before, within Jewish philosophical and gnostic circles that were open to Greco-Roman ideas. Jesus tells Judas that in the beginning there was an infinite, utterly transcendent deity, and through a complex series of emanations and creations, the heavens became filled with divine light and glory. This infinite deity is so exalted that no finite term can adequately describe the deity; even the word *God,* it is intimated, is insufficient and inappropriate for the deity. The world below, however, is the domain of a lower ruler, a creator god named Nebro ("Rebel") or Yaldabaoth, who is malevolent and mean-spirited—hence the problems in our world, and hence the need to listen to words of wisdom and become aware of the divine light within. For these believers, the most profound mystery of the universe is that within some human beings is the spirit of the divine. Although we live in a flawed world that too often is the domain of darkness and death, we can transcend darkness and embrace life. We are better than this world, Jesus explains to Judas, for we belong to the world of the divine. If Jesus is the son of the divine, so also are all of us children of the divine. All we need to do is live out of that knowledge of the divine, and we shall be enlightened.

In contrast to the New Testament gospels, Judas Iscariot is presented as a thoroughly positive figure in the Gospel of Judas, a role model for all those who wish to be disciples of Jesus. That is probably why the Gospel of Judas ends with the story of the betrayal of Jesus and not the crucifixion of Jesus. The point of the gospel is the insight and loyalty of Judas as the paradigm of discipleship. In the end, he does exactly what Jesus wants. In the biblical tradition, however, Judas—whose name has been linked to "Jew" and "Judaism"—was often portrayed as the evil Jew who turned Jesus in to be arrested and killed, and thereby the biblical figure of Judas the Betrayer has fed the flames of anti-Semitism. Judas in the present gospel may counteract this anti-Semitic tendency. He does nothing Jesus himself does not ask him to do, and he listens to Jesus and remains faithful to him. In the Gospel of Judas, Judas Iscariot turns out to be Jesus' beloved disciple and dear friend. Additionally, the mysteries he learns from Jesus are steeped in Jewish gnostic lore, and the teacher of these mysteries, Jesus, is the master, the rabbi. The Christian Gospel of Judas is at peace with a Jewish view—an alternative Jewish view, to be sure—of gnostic thought, and Jewish gnostic thought has been baptized as Christian gnostic thought.

In this book, Jesus echoes the Platonic conviction that every person has his or her own star and that the fate of people is connected to their stars. Judas, Jesus says, also has his star. Near the conclusion of the text, just before Judas is transfigured and enlightened in a luminous cloud, Jesus asks Judas to look up at the heavens and see the stars and the display of light. There are many stars in the sky, but the star of Judas is special. As Jesus tells Judas, "The star that leads the way is your star."

The present volume offers the first publication of the Gospel of Judas in modern times. This is the first known appearance of this remarkable gospel since it was read in the early Church and eventually hidden away in Egypt. The Gospel of Judas was apparently discovered, as the third text in a papyrus codex (or book) now designated Codex Tchacos, in the 1970s in Middle Egypt. It is preserved in Coptic translation, though without a doubt it was composed in Greek, probably around the middle of the second century. This date becomes more secure on the basis of a statement of the early church father Irenaeus of Lyon, who referred to a Gospel of Judas in his work *Against Heresies,* written around 180. As Gregor Wurst demonstrates in his essay, the Gospel of Judas mentioned by Irenaeus and others after him may now be identified as a version of the Gospel of Judas in Codex Tchacos. The Coptic translation of the Gospel of Judas is most likely somewhat older than the copy in Codex Tchacos, which probably dates to the early part of the fourth century, though the carbon-14 dating would also allow for a slightly earlier date for the codex.

The English translation of the Gospel of Judas published here is based on the collaborative work of Rodolphe Kasser, Marvin Meyer, and Gregor Wurst, along with François Gaudard. Rodolphe Kasser,

Professor Emeritus in the Faculty of Arts at the University of Geneva, Switzerland, is widely published in Coptic studies, and he has edited several important Greek and Coptic codices. Marvin Meyer, Griset Professor of Bible and Christian Studies at Chapman University, Orange, California, has focused much of his scholarly research on the texts of the Nag Hammadi library. Gregor Wurst, Professor of the History of Christianity in the Faculty of Catholic Theology of the University of Augsburg, Germany, does research and publishing in Coptic and Manichaean studies. François Gaudard, research associate at the Oriental Institute of the University of Chicago, is a scholar of Coptic and Demotic. Beginning in 2001, Professor Kasser undertook, with conservator Florence Darbre and (since 2004) Professor Wurst, the herculean task of assembling and arranging the papyrus fragments, large and small, of a codex that required significant reconstruction. A consensus English translation of the recovered text of the Gospel of Judas, with which all the translators are in essential agreement, is published in this volume.

Within the translation, the numbers of the manuscript pages are given in square brackets ([...]), and in the accompanying discussions, sections of the text are referred to by these page numbers. Square brackets are also used to indicate lacunae (gaps in the text due to loss of ink or loss of papyrus), with restorations of lacunae placed within the brackets. Occasionally names or words that are partially restored are placed partly inside and partly outside square brackets, in order to indicate the portion of the name or word that survives in the manuscript. When a short lacuna of less than a manuscript line cannot be restored with confidence, three ellipsis dots are placed within the brackets. For unrestored lacunae longer than a fraction of a manuscript line, the approximate number of missing lines is indicated within the square brackets. Because of the fragmentary nature of the manuscript and portions of the text that remain unaccounted for, there are several rather long lacunae, with a substantial number of lines missing. Once in a while, angled brackets (< ... >) are used for an emendation of an error in the text. Alternative translations and particular issues of translation are indicated in the footnotes.

The entire text of Codex Tchacos is to be published in a critical edition, with facsimile photographs, Coptic text, English, French, and German translations, textual notes, introductions, indices, and an essay on Coptic dialectical features. As far as we can tell, Codex Tchacos is a book sixty-six pages long with four tractates:

- a version of the Letter of Peter to Philip (pages 1–9), also known from Nag Hammadi Codex VIII

- a text entitled "James" (pages 10–32), which is a version of the First Revelation of James from Nag Hammadi Codex V
- the Gospel of Judas (pages 33–58)
- a text provisionally entitled the Book of Allogenes (or, the Stranger, an epithet of Seth, son of Adam and Eve, in gnostic texts), previously unknown (pages 59–66)

The codex was acquired by the Maecenas Foundation for Ancient Art in 2000 and shown to Rodolphe Kasser in the summer of 2001. Kasser reported on his continuing work on the Gospel of Judas and Codex Tchacos in 2004 at the Eighth Congress of the International Association for Coptic Studies in Paris. Since then, there has been considerable interest in and speculation about the Gospel of Judas, and we publish it here in order to make it available as quickly as possible.

As this volume was going to press, another portion of a papyrus folio of the Gospel of Judas, representing the lower parts of pages 37 and 38, was located and brought to our attention. We produced, as quickly as we could, a transcription and translation of the Coptic text on these pages, although we were unable to reflect upon these passages in the essays included in the commentary. As will be noted in the translation, the section of the

Gospel of Judas on the bottom of page 37 continues to describe the scene of Jesus with the disciples before they see the Temple. After Jesus concludes his statement and the disciples become troubled by what he has said, the text indicates that Jesus comes to the disciples once again, on another day, for another conversation. The section on the bottom of page 38 has the disciples responding to a question of Jesus by apparently reflecting, in a polemical way, upon supposed misdeeds of the priests in the Temple with comments that anticipate the allegorical interpretation of the vision of the Temple and those in it given by Jesus on pages 39 and following. The placement of this large fragment of papyrus, while making the text of the Gospel of Judas that much more complete, also brings greater clarity to the storyline and the message of this fascinating gospel.

The translation of the Gospel of Judas is presented in such a way as to enhance the understanding of the text. Subtitles within the translation, not found in the text itself, are provided by the translators in order to clarify the translation, structure, and flow of the text. A substantial set of footnotes accompanies the translation. In the commentary of the gospel that follows, essays by Rodolphe Kasser, Bart Ehrman, Gregor Wurst, and Marvin Meyer offer suggestions for how the Gospel of Judas may be interpreted. Rodolphe Kasser discusses the story of Codex Tchacos and the recovery of the Gospel of Judas. Bart Ehrman, James A. Gray Distinguished Professor and Chair of Religious Studies at the University of North Carolina, provides an overview of the alternative spiritual vision of the Gospel of Judas. Gregor Wurst evaluates the statements by Irenaeus of Lyon and other heresiologists on the Gospel of Judas in the light of the present text. Marvin Meyer offers a more detailed analysis of the Sethian gnostic features of the text and relates these features to other religious literature in the world of the early Church. These essays expand upon the issues that are confronted in the Gospel of Judas, and they may help to clarify various points of interpretation. Some of the essays include notes, published at the conclusion of the volume, with suggestions for further interpretation and additional reading. The notes are listed with references to the pages and lines in the essays where the issues of interest are discussed.

After being lost for sixteen hundred years or longer, the Gospel of Judas has at last been found. The authors of this volume hope that the Gospel of Judas may contribute to our knowledge and appreciation of the history, development, and diversity of the early Church and shed light on the enduring issues faced in that formative period.

—*Marvin Meyer*

THE GOSPEL OF JUDAS

Translated by
Rodolphe Kasser, Marvin Meyer, and Gregor Wurst,
in collaboration with François Gaudard

THE GOSPEL OF JUDAS

INTRODUCTION: INCIPIT

The secret account[1] of the revelation[2] that Jesus spoke in conversation with Judas Iscariot during a week[3] three days before he celebrated Passover.[4]

---

[1] Or, "treatise," "discourse," "word" (Coptic, from Greek, *logos*). The opening of the text may also be translated to read "The secret revelatory word" or "The secret explanatory word." A substantial number of words of Greek derivation are included in the Coptic text of the Gospel of Judas as loanwords.

[2] Or, "declaration," "exposition," "statement" (Coptic, from Greek, *apophasis*). In his *Refutation of All Heresies* (6.9.4–18.7), Hippolytus of Rome cites another work, attributed to Simon Magus, that employs the same Greek term in its title: *Apophasis megalē*—Great Revelation (or, Declaration, Exposition, Statement). The incipit, or opening of the present text, reads "The Secret Account of the Revelation of Jesus" (or the like). The titular subscript, "The Gospel of Judas," is found at the end of the text.

[3] Literally, "during eight days," probably intended to indicate a week.

[4] Or, perhaps, but much less likely, "three days before his passion." The Gospel of Judas chronicles events described as taking place over a short period of time leading up to the betrayal of Jesus by Judas. In the New Testament, cf. Matthew 21:1–26:56; Mark 11:1–14:52; Luke 19:28–22:53; John 12:12–18:11.

The Earthly Ministry of Jesus

When Jesus appeared on earth, he performed miracles and great wonders for the salvation of humanity. And since some [walked] in the way of righteousness while others walked in their transgressions, the twelve disciples were called.[5]

He began to speak with them about the mysteries[6] beyond the world and what would take place at the end. Often he did not appear to his disciples as himself, but he was found among them as a child.[7]

SCENE I: *Jesus dialogues with his disciples: The prayer of thanksgiving or the eucharist*

One day he was with his disciples in Judea, and he found them gathered together and seated in pious observance.[8] When he [approached] his disciples, [34]

---

[5] On the calling of the twelve disciples, cf. Matthew 10:1–4; Mark 3:13–19; Luke 6:12–16.

[6] Coptic, from Greek, *emmustērion*, here and in subsequent text.

[7] Sahidic Coptic *hrot*, which we take as a form of the Bohairic Coptic word *hrot*, "child." Much less likely is the possibility that *hrot* may be a form of the Bohairic Coptic word *hortef*, "apparition." On Jesus appearing as a child, cf. Secret Book of John (Nag Hammadi Codex II), 2; Revelation of Paul 18; Hippolytus of Rome *Refutation of All Heresies* 6.42.2, where Hippolytus reports a story that the Word (*Logos*) appeared to Valentinus as a child; Gospel of Thomas 4. On Jesus appearing as an apparition, cf. the Acts of John, the Second Discourse of Great Seth, and the Nag Hammadi Revelation of Peter.

[8] Literally, "training (or practicing) their piety" (Coptic, partly from Greek, *euergumnaze etmntnoute*; cf. 1 Timothy 4:7).

gathered together and seated and offering a prayer of thanksgiving[9] over the bread, [he] laughed.[10]

The disciples said to [him], "Master, why are you laughing at [our] prayer of thanksgiving?[11] We have done what is right."[12]

He answered and said to them, "I am not laughing at you. <You> are not doing this because of your own will but because it is through this that your god [will be] praised."[13]

They said, "Master, you are [...] the son of our god."[14]

Jesus said to them, "How do you know me? Truly [I] say to you,[15] no generation of the people that are among you will know me."[16]

---

[9] Coptic, from Greek, *euͤreukharisti*.

[10] The scene recalls, in part, accounts of the Last Supper, particularly the blessing over the bread, or descriptions of some other holy meal within Judaism and Christianity. The specific language used here calls to mind even more the celebration of the eucharist within Christianity; cf. additional criticisms within the Gospel of Judas of forms of worship within the emerging orthodox Church. On Jesus laughing, cf. Second Discourse of Great Seth 56; Revelation of Peter 81; several other passages in the Gospel of Judas.

[11] Or, "eucharist" (Coptic, from Greek, *eukharistia*).

[12] Or, "Have we not done what is right?"

[13] Or, "[will receive] thanksgiving." It is also possible to translate this clause as a question: "But is it through this that your god [will be] praised?" The god described as the god of the disciples is not the exalted deity above but rather the ruler of this world.

[14] Cf. the confession of Peter in Matthew 16:13–20, Mark 8:27–30, and Luke 9:18–21. Here, however, the disciples mistakenly confess that Jesus is the son of their own god.

[15] Or, "Amen I say to you." This is the standard introductory statement of authority in sayings of Jesus in early Christian literature. Here and elsewhere in the Gospel of Judas, the statement is given with the Coptic *hamēn* (from the Hebrew *'amen*).

[16] In the Gospel of Judas and other Sethian texts, the human generations are distinguished from "that generation" (Coptic *tgenea etͤmmau*), the great generation of Seth—that is, the gnostics. Only those of "that generation" know the true nature of Jesus. Elsewhere in Sethian literature—for example, in the Revelation of Adam—the people of Seth can similarly be described as "those people" (Coptic *nirōme etͤmmau*).

The Disciples Become Angry

When his disciples heard this, they started getting angry and infuriated and began blaspheming against him in their hearts.

When Jesus observed their lack of [understanding, he said] to them, "Why has this agitation led you to anger? Your god who is within you and [...][17] [35] have provoked you to anger [within] your souls. [Let] any one of you who is [strong enough] among human beings bring out the perfect human and stand before my face."[18]

They all said, "We have the strength."

But their spirits[19] did not dare to stand before [him], except for Judas Iscariot. He was able to stand before him, but he could not look him in the eyes, and he turned his face away.[20]

Judas [said] to him, "I know who you are and where you have come from. You are from the immortal realm[21]

---

[17] Perhaps "[his powers]," or the like.

[18] The restoration is tentative. Here Jesus indicates that the anger rising within the hearts of the disciples is being provoked by their god within them. Jesus challenges them to allow the true person—the spiritual person—to come to expression and stand before him.

[19] Here and elsewhere in the text, "spirit" apparently means "living being"; cf. Gospel of Judas 43, 53.

[20] Of the disciples, only Judas has the strength to stand before Jesus, and he does so with modesty and respect. On Judas averting his eyes before Jesus, cf. Gospel of Thomas 46, where it is said that people should show a similar form of modesty by lowering the eyes before John the Baptizer.

[21] Or, "aeon," here and in subsequent text.

of Barbelo.[22] And I am not worthy to utter the name of the one who has sent you."[23]

JESUS SPEAKS TO JUDAS PRIVATELY

Knowing that Judas was reflecting upon something that was exalted, Jesus said to him, "Step away from the others and I shall tell you the mysteries of the kingdom.[24] It is possible for you to reach it, but you will grieve a great deal. [36] For someone else will replace you, in order that the twelve [disciples] may again come to completion with their god."[25]

Judas said to him, "When will you tell me these things, and [when][26] will the great day of light dawn for the generation?"

---

[22] In the Gospel of Judas, it is Judas himself who provides the true confession of who Jesus is. To confess that Jesus is from the immortal realm (or aeon) of Barbelo is to profess, in Sethian terms, that Jesus is from the divine realm above and is the son of God. In Sethian texts, Barbelo is the divine Mother of all, who often is said to be the Forethought (*pronoia*) of the Father, the infinite One. The name of Barbelo seems to be based on a form of the tetragrammaton, the holy four-letter name of God within Judaism, and it apparently comes from Hebrew—perhaps "God (compare *El*) in (*b-*) four (*arb(a)*)." For presentations of Barbelo in Sethian literature, see Secret Book of John II:4–5; Holy Book of the Great Invisible Spirit (also known as the Egyptian Gospel; Nag Hammadi Codex III) 42, 62, 69; Zostrianos 14, 124, 129; Allogenes the Stranger 51, 53, 56; Three Forms of First Thought 38.

[23] The one who has sent Jesus is the ineffable God. The ineffability of the divine is also asserted in Gospel of Judas 47, and it is emphasized in such Sethian texts as the Secret Book of John, the Holy Book of the Great Invisible Spirit, and Allogenes the Stranger. In Gospel of Thomas 13, Thomas similarly declares to Jesus, "Teacher, my mouth is utterly unable to say what you are like."

[24] Or, "reign"—that is, the kingdom or reign of God.

[25] Cf. Acts 1:15–26, on the selection of Matthias to replace Judas in the circle of the twelve in order to complete the twelve once again.

[26] Or, "[how]."

But when he said this, Jesus left him.[27]

SCENE 2: *Jesus appears to the disciples again*

The next morning, after this happened,[28] Jesus [appeared] to his disciples again.[29]

They said to him, "Master, where did you go and what did you do when you left us?"

Jesus said to them, "I went to another great and holy generation."[30]

His disciples said to him, "Lord, what is the great generation that is superior to us and holier than us, that is not now in these realms?"[31]

When Jesus heard this, he laughed and said to them, "Why are you thinking in your hearts about the strong and holy generation? [37] Truly[32] [I] say to you, no one born [of] this aeon will see that [generation], and no host of angels of the stars will rule over that generation, and no person of mortal birth can associate with it,

---

[27] Judas asks questions about the promised revelation from Jesus and the ultimate glorification of that generation, but Jesus abruptly leaves.

[28] Or, "At dawn of the next day."

[29] The word "again" is implied in the text.

[30] Jesus maintains that he went beyond this world to another realm, apparently the spiritual realm of that generation.

[31] These realms or aeons are the ones, here below, that are mere copies or reflections of the realms or aeons above. This theme is discussed more fully later in the text. The Platonic character of this theme is clear, but the Platonic concept of the realm of ideas and the reflections of ideas in our world is interpreted in a gnostic manner in the Gospel of Judas and other texts, especially Sethian texts.

[32] Amen.

because that generation does not come from [...] which has become [...]. The generation of people among [you] is from the generation of humanity [...] power, which [... the] other powers [...] by [which] you rule."[33]

When [his] disciples heard this, they each were troubled in spirit. They could not say a word.

Another day Jesus came up to [them]. They said to [him], "Master, we have seen you in a [vision], for we have had great [dreams ...] night [...]."[34]

[He said], "Why have [you ... when] <you> have gone into hiding?"[35] [38]

The Disciples See the Temple and Discuss It

They[36] [said, "We have seen] a great [house with a large] altar [in it, and] twelve men—they are the

---

[33] In this passage Jesus seems to say, among other things, that the great generation comes from above and is indomitable, and that people who are part of this world below live in mortality and cannot attain that great generation.

[34] Here the text may be restored, tentatively, as follows: "for we have had great [dreams of the] night on which they have come to [arrest you]," in which case the disciples may be referring to premonitions of the arrest of Jesus in the Garden of Gethsemane.

[35] If the restoration proposed in the last note is accepted, this may be a reference to the disciples running away to hide, in terror, when Jesus is arrested. Cf. Matthew 26:56; Mark 14:50–52.

[36] Here the text suggests that the disciples have a vision of the Jewish Temple in Jerusalem—or, less likely, that they have gone to visit the Temple—and then they report on what they have seen (cf. pronouns in the first-person plural "we" in this passage). In the section that follows, Jesus refers explicitly to what the disciples "have seen"; this provides part of the justification for the restoration of lacunae proposed in this section. In the New Testament gospels, cf. the accounts of the visits of Jesus and the disciples to the Temple in Matthew 21:12–17, 24:1–25:46; Mark 11:15–19, 13:1–37; Luke 19:45–48, 21:5–38; and John 2:13–22.

priests, we would say—and a name;[37] and a crowd of people is waiting at that altar,[38] [until] the priests [... and receive] the offerings. [But] we kept waiting."

[Jesus said], "What are [the priests][39] like?"

They [said, "Some[40] ...] two weeks; [some] sacrifice their own children, others their wives, in praise [and][41] humility with each other; some sleep with men; some are involved in [slaughter];[42] some commit a multitude of sins and deeds of lawlessness. And the men who stand [before] the altar invoke your [name], [39] and in all the deeds of their deficiency,[43] the sacrifices are brought to completion [...]."

After they said this, they were quiet, for they were troubled.

JESUS OFFERS AN ALLEGORICAL INTERPRETATION OF THE VISION OF THE TEMPLE

---

[37] Apparently the name of Jesus; cf. Gospel of Judas 38 ("your [name]") and 39 ("my name"). In the context of the Jewish Temple in Jerusalem, the reference to "a name" could also be understood to refer to the ineffable name of God (Yahweh) in Judaism.

[38] Here the text seems inadvertently to repeat "to the altar" (a case of dittography).

[39] The restoration is tentative but reasonable in the context.

[40] On this section, cf. the polemical description of leaders of the emerging orthodox Church in the allegorical interpretation of the vision of the Temple given by Jesus in Gospel of Judas 39–40.

[41] Or, "[or]."

[42] The restoration is tentative.

[43] "Deficiency" (Coptic *šōōt*) is a technical word in Sethian and other texts for the lack of divine light and knowledge that can be traced to the fall of the Mother—usually Sophia, the Wisdom of God—and the subsequent loss of enlightenment. Cf., for example, Letter of Peter to Philip 3–4 (Codex Tchacos), 135 (Nag Hammadi Codex VIII). This passage is quoted in the commentary of this book. On corruptible Sophia, cf. Gospel of Judas 44.

Jesus said to them, "Why are you troubled? Truly[44] I say to you, all the priests who stand before that altar invoke my name. Again I say to you, my name has been written on this [...] of the generations of the stars through the human generations. [And they] have planted trees without fruit, in my name, in a shameful manner."[45]

Jesus said to them, "Those you have seen receiving the offerings at the altar—that is who you are.[46] That is the god you serve, and you are those twelve men you have seen. The cattle you have seen brought for sacrifice are the many people you lead astray [40] before that altar. [...][47] will stand and make use of my name in this way, and generations of the pious will remain loyal to him. After him[48] another man will stand there from[49] [the fornicators], and another [will] stand there from

[44] Amen.

[45] The reference to planting trees without fruit, in the name of Jesus, seems to be an indictment of those who preach in the name of Jesus but proclaim a gospel without fruitful content. The same image of trees bearing or not bearing fruit is found in Revelation of Adam 76, 85; cf. Gospel of Judas 43. Also compare, perhaps, the withered fig tree in Matthew 21:18–19 and Mark 11:12–14.

[46] Throughout this section, Jesus interprets what the disciples have seen at the Temple as a metaphor for erroneous religious instruction, apparently in the emerging orthodox Church. The priests are the disciples, and perhaps their successors in the Church, and the animals led to the slaughter are the victims of the improper religious observance in the Church.

[47] Perhaps "[The ruler (or archon) of this world]"; cf. 1 Corinthians 2:8.

[48] Or, but less likely, "After that."

[49] Coptic, from Greek, parista (two lines later, parhista). The people who stand may be leaders in the emerging orthodox Church who are judged, in this polemical section, to be working as assistants of the ruler of this world. The verb may also be translated as "represent," here and in the passages that follow, rather than "stand there from."

the slayers of children,[50] and another from those who sleep[51] with men, and those who abstain,[52] and the rest of the people of pollution and lawlessness and error, and those who say, 'We are like angels'; they are the stars that bring everything to its conclusion. For to the human generations it has been said, 'Look, God has received your sacrifice from the hands of a priest'—that is, a minister of error. But it is the Lord, the Lord of the universe,[53] who commands, 'On the last day they will be put to shame.'"[54] [41]

Jesus said [to them], "Stop sac[rificing ...] which you have [...] over the altar, since they are over your stars and your angels and have already come to their conclusion there.[55] So let them be [ensnared][56] before you, and let them go [—about 15 lines missing—][57]

---

[50] Here the text seems to suggest that the leaders of the emerging orthodox Church are immoral in their own lives and are endangering the lives of the children of God and leading them into spiritual death. This image may recall the comparison with cattle being led to death in temple sacrifice.

[51] Here we read *nrefnkotk* for the *nrefnkokt* of the manuscript. The accusation of sexual impropriety is a standard feature of polemical argumentation. One's opponents are frequently said to be immoral people.

[52] Or, "fast." For a similar negative view of fasting, cf. Gospel of Thomas 6.

[53] Or, "All," that is, the fullness of the divine realm above (Coptic *ptēr*f).

[54] At the end of time, the leaders of the emerging orthodox Church will be punished for their acts of impiety.

[55] Here Jesus seems to indicate that the leaders of the emerging orthodox Church are strong, but their time is coming to an end.

[56] Or, "entrapped," "upbraided." The reading and meaning of the text are uncertain. The Coptic (apparently *šōnt*, literally "entwined") may also be translated "quarreling" or "in a struggle."

[57] An extant photograph from an earlier inspection of the codex, though lacking in clarity, reveals a few words and expressions.

generations […]. A baker cannot feed all creation [42] under [heaven].[58] And […] to them […] and […] to us and […].

Jesus said to them, "Stop struggling with me. Each of you has his own star,[59] and every[body—*about 17 lines missing*—] [43] in […] who[60] has come [… spring] for the tree[61] […] of this aeon […] for a time […] but he[62] has come to water God's paradise,[63] and the [generation][64] that will last, because [he] will not defile the [walk of life of] that generation, but […] for all eternity."[65]

JUDAS ASKS JESUS ABOUT THAT GENERATION AND HUMAN GENERATIONS

---

[58] This statement may be an ancient proverb about setting reasonable goals for what people can accomplish—in this case, readers of the Gospel of Judas who face the opposition of the emerging orthodox Church. Conversely, the statement may also be intended as a critique of the eucharist as it is celebrated in the emerging orthodox Church.

[59] The teaching here and elsewhere in the Gospel of Judas that each person has a star seems to reflect Plato's presentation in his *Timaeus*. After a statement by the creator of the world, it is said there that the creator "assigned each soul to a star" and declared that "the person who lived well during his appointed time was to return and dwell in his native star" (41d–42b; the passage is quoted at length in the commentary of this book). On the star of Judas, cf. Gospel of Judas 57.

[60] Or, "which."

[61] The reference to a tree, in this fragmentary portion of the text, may indicate one of the trees in paradise. The trees of the Garden of Eden are frequently discussed in gnostic texts, and the tree of the knowledge (Greek *gnōsis*) of good and evil is often thought to be a source of the knowledge of God. Cf. Secret Book of John II:22–23.

[62] Or, "it." The identity of the pronominal subject here and in the next lines is uncertain.

[63] Cf. Genesis 2:10.

[64] Or, "race." Here and elsewhere in the text, rather than the Coptic *genea*, which is usually employed, the Coptic reads *genos*. Both words derive from Greek.

[65] Literally, "from everlasting to everlasting."

Judas said to [him, "Rabb]i,[66] what kind of fruit does this generation produce?"[67]

Jesus said, "The souls of every human generation will die. When these people, however, have completed the time of the kingdom and the spirit[68] leaves them, their bodies will die but their souls will be alive, and they will be taken up."

Judas said, "And what will the rest of the human generations do?"

Jesus said, "It is impossible [44] to sow seed on [rock] and harvest its fruit.[69] [This] is also the way [...] the [defiled] generation[70] [...] and corruptible Sophia[71] [...] the hand that has created mortal people, so that their souls go up to the eternal realms above. [Truly][72] I say to you, [...] angel [...] power[73] will be able to see that [...] these to whom [...] holy generations [...]."

After Jesus said this, he departed.

---

[66] The title "rabbi" (largely restored) is the Hebrew term for a Jewish teacher or master.
[67] Compare and contrast Gospel of Judas 39, on those who plant trees without fruit.
[68] The spirit or breath of life? On spirit and soul, cf. also Gospel of Judas 53.
[69] Cf. the parable of the sower in Matthew 13:1–23, Mark 4:1–20, Luke 8:4–15, and Gospel of Thomas 9. According to the parable, seed that is sown and lands on rock cannot take root and thus cannot produce heads of grain.
[70] Or, "race," as above.
[71] Or, "Wisdom," that part of the divine, in gnostic tradition, that falls through a lapse of wisdom and is eventually restored to the fullness of the divine once again. Sophia is often personified as a female figure in Jewish and Christian literature, and she plays a central role in many gnostic texts, including Sethian texts. Cf., for example, the account of the fall of Sophia in Secret Book of John II:9–10, which is cited in the commentary of this book. The child of Sophia, according to gnostic accounts, is the demiurge Saklas or Yaldabaoth. Cf. Gospel of Judas 51.
[72] Amen.
[73] Perhaps, "angel [of the great] power."

SCENE 3: *Judas recounts a vision and Jesus responds*

Judas said, "Master, as you have listened to all of them, now also listen to me. For I have seen a great vision."

When Jesus heard this, he laughed and said to him, "You thirteenth spirit,[74] why do you try so hard? But speak up, and I shall bear with you."

Judas said to him, "In the vision I saw myself as the twelve disciples were stoning me and {45} persecuting [me severely]. And I also came to the place where [...] after you. I saw [a house ...],[75] and my eyes could not [comprehend] its size. Great people were surrounding it, and that house <had> a roof of greenery,[76] and in the middle of the house was [a crowd—*two lines missing*—], saying,[77] 'Master, take me in along with these people.'"

[Jesus] answered and said, "Judas, your star has led you astray." He continued, "No person of mortal birth is worthy to enter the house you have seen, for that place

---

[74] Or, "thirteenth demon" (Coptic, from Greek, *daimōn*). Judas is thirteenth because he is the disciple excluded from the circle of the twelve, and he is a demon (or daemon) because his true identity is spiritual. Compare tales of Socrates and his *daimōn* or *daimonion*, in Plato *Symposium* 202e–203a.

[75] Judas reports a vision in which he is harshly opposed by the other disciples (cf. Gospel of Judas 35–36, 46–47). In the vision, Judas approaches a place and makes mention of Jesus ("after you"); there is a great heavenly house there, and Judas asks that he may be received into that house along with the others who are entering. On the heavenly house or mansion, cf. John 14:1–14. On the eventual ascension or transfiguration of Judas, cf. Gospel of Judas 57–58.

[76] The reading is conjectural and corrects an obvious scribal error.

[77] The word "saying" is implied in the text.

is reserved for the holy.[78] Neither the sun nor the moon will rule there, nor the day, but the holy will abide[79] there always, in the eternal realm with the holy angels.[80] Look, I have explained to you the mysteries of the kingdom [46] and I have taught you about the error of the stars; and [...] send it [...] on the twelve aeons."

JUDAS ASKS ABOUT HIS OWN FATE

Judas said, "Master, could it be that my seed[81] is under the control of the rulers?"[82]

Jesus answered and said to him, "Come, that I [—*two lines missing*—], but that you will grieve much when you see the kingdom and all its generation."

When he heard this, Judas said to him, "What good is it that I have received it? For you have set me apart for that generation."

Jesus answered and said, "You will become the thirteenth,[83]

---

[78] Or, "the saints," here and in subsequent text.

[79] Or, "stand."

[80] On this apocalyptic description of heaven, cf. Revelation 21:23. According to Secret Book of John II:9, the souls of the holy or the saints dwell in the third eternal realm, with the third luminary Daveithai, the home of the offspring of Seth. Cf. also Holy Book of the Great Invisible Spirit III:50–51.

[81] The seed is the spiritual part of a person, the spark of the divine within, and, collectively, the offspring of those who come from the divine. Thus, in Sethian texts gnostics can be called the seed or offspring of Seth.

[82] Or, "archons," here and in subsequent text—that is, the rulers of this world, especially the cosmic powers who collaborate with the demiurge. This clause may also be translated "that my seed subdues the rulers?"

[83] On Judas as the thirteenth, cf. Gospel of Judas 44, where Judas is said to be the thirteenth spirit or demon.

and you will be cursed by the other generations—and you will come to rule over them.[84] In the last days they will curse your ascent[85] [47] to the holy [generation]."

JESUS TEACHES JUDAS ABOUT COSMOLOGY: THE SPIRIT AND THE SELF-GENERATED

Jesus said, "[Come], that I may teach you about [secrets][86] no person [has] ever seen. For there exists a great and boundless realm, whose extent no generation of angels has seen, [in which] there is [a] great invisible [Spirit],[87]

which no eye of an angel has ever seen,
no thought of the heart has ever comprehended,
and it was never called by any name.[88]

---

[84] On Judas being cursed, compare the assessments of Judas in Matthew 26:20–25, 27:3–10; Mark 14:17–21; Luke 22:21–23; John 13:21–30; and Acts 1:15–20. Here it is suggested that Judas is despised by the other disciples, but he is to be exalted over them as the preeminent disciple.

[85] Or, "return up." The translation is tentative. The text seems to allude to some kind of transformation or ascent, as in Gospel of Judas 57 (the transfiguration of Judas) or 2 Corinthians 12:2–4 (the ecstatic ascent of a man—Paul—to the third heaven).

[86] Or, "hidden things." The restoration is tentative. For a full account of Sethian cosmology, cf. Secret Book of John and Holy Book of the Great Invisible Spirit.

[87] Or, "[the] great invisible [Spirit]." In many Sethian texts—for example, the Secret Book of John and the Holy Book of the Great Invisible Spirit—the transcendent deity is called the great invisible Spirit.

[88] Cf. 1 Corinthians 2:9; Gospel of Thomas 17; Prayer of the Apostle Paul A. The parallel text in the Valentinian Prayer of the Apostle Paul is close to part of the formulation in the Gospel of Judas: "Grant what eyes of angels have not [seen], what ears of rulers have not heard, and what has not arisen in the human heart, which became angelic, made in the image of the animate god when it was formed in the beginning." The ineffability and transcendence of the divine is emphasized in many gnostic texts, especially Sethian texts. Cf. Secret Book of John II:2–4; Holy

"And a luminous cloud[89] appeared there. He[90] said, 'Let an angel[91] come into being as my attendant.'[92]

"A great angel, the enlightened divine Self-Generated,[93] emerged from the cloud. Because of him, four other angels came into being from another cloud, and they became attendants[94] for the angelic Self-Generated.[95] The Self-Generated said, [48] 'Let [...] come into being [...],' and it came into being [...]. And he [created] the first luminary[96] to reign over him. He said, 'Let angels come into being to serve [him],'[97] and myriads without number came into being. He said,

---

Book of the Great Invisible Spirit III:40–41; Allogenes the Stranger; Irenaeus of Lyon *Against Heresies* 1.29.1–4, on the "gnostics" or "Barbelognostics" ("gnostics of Barbelo"); Gospel of Judas 35. Lines from the Secret Book of John illustrating such descriptions of divine transcendence are quoted in the commentary of this book.

[89] Or, "cloud of light." The luminous cloud is a manifestation of the glorious heavenly presence of the divine, and clouds of light often appear in ancient descriptions of theophanies. In the accounts of the transfiguration of Jesus in the New Testament gospels, for instance, luminous clouds accompany the revelation of glory (Matthew 17:5–6; Mark 9:7–8; Luke 9:34–35). In the Holy Book of the Great Invisible Spirit, heavenly clouds also play an important role; in the Secret Book of John, there is light surrounding the Father of All.

[90] The Spirit.

[91] Or, "messenger," here and in subsequent text.

[92] Or, "as my assistant," "to stand by me" (Coptic, from Greek, *parastasis*). Compare the verb *parista/parhista* in Gospel of Judas 40.

[93] Or, "Self-Begotten," "Self-Engendered," "Self-Conceived," "Autogenes" (Coptic *autogenēs*, from Greek), here and in subsequent text. Typically the Self-Generated is the child of God in Sethian texts; cf. Secret Book of John II:7–9; Holy Book of the Great Invisible Spirit III:49, IV:60; Zostrianos 6, 7, 127; Allogenes the Stranger 46, 51, 58.

[94] Again, Coptic, from Greek, *parastasis*.

[95] In Secret Book of John II:7–8, the Four Luminaries, named Harmozel, Oroiael, Daveithai, and Eleleth, come into being through the Self-Generated. Cf. also Holy Book of the Great Invisible Spirit III:51–53; Zostrianos 127–28; Three Forms of First Thought 38–39.

[96] Coptic, from Greek, *phōstēr*, here and in subsequent text.

[97] Or, "offer adoration," "offer worship" (Coptic *šᵉmše*, here and in subsequent text).

'[Let] an enlightened aeon[98] come into being,' and he came into being. He created the second luminary [to] reign over him, together with myriads of angels without number, to offer service. That is how he created the rest of the enlightened aeons. He made them reign over them, and he created for them myriads of angels without number, to assist them.[99]

Adamas and the Luminaries

"Adamas[100] was in the first luminous cloud[101] that no angel has ever seen among all those called 'God.' He [49] [...] that [...] the image [...] and after the likeness of [this] angel. He made the incorruptible [generation] of Seth[102] appear [...] the twelve [...] the twenty-four [...]. He made seventy-two luminaries appear in the incorruptible generation, in accordance with the will of the Spirit. The seventy-two luminaries themselves made

---

[98] Or, "an aeon of light."

[99] According to the text, the divine realm is filled with luminaries, aeons, and angels brought into being by the creative word of the Self-Generated, to serve and adore the divine.

[100] Adamas is Adam, the first human of Genesis, here understood, as in many other gnostic texts, to be the paradigmatic human of the divine realm and the exalted image of humanity. Cf., for example, Secret Book of John II:8–9.

[101] The first luminous cloud is the initial manifestation of the divine; cf. Gospel of Judas 47.

[102] This is Seth, son of Adam, also in the divine realm; cf. Genesis 4:25–5:8. The role of Seth as the progenitor of the generation of Seth ("that generation") is well established in Sethian texts; cf. also Gospel of Judas 52.

three hundred sixty luminaries appear in the incorruptible generation, in accordance with the will of the Spirit, that their number should be five for each.[103]

"The twelve aeons of the twelve luminaries constitute their father, with six heavens for each aeon, so that there are seventy-two heavens for the seventy-two luminaries, and for each [50] [of them five] firmaments, [for a total of] three hundred sixty [firmaments ...]. They were given authority and a [great] host of angels [without number], for glory and adoration, [and after that also] virgin[104] spirits,[105] for glory and [adoration] of all the aeons and the heavens and their firmaments.[106]

THE COSMOS, CHAOS, AND THE UNDERWORLD

"The multitude of those immortals is called the cosmos—

---

[103] Everything finally happens in accordance with the will of the divine, the Spirit.

[104] In Sethian texts, the term *virgin* is used as an epithet for a variety of divine manifestations and powers in order to stress their purity. In the Holy Book of the Great Invisible Spirit, for example, the great invisible Spirit, Barbelo, Youel, and Plesithea are described as virgins, and additional mention is made of more virgins.

[105] Eugnostos the Blessed includes a passage on the aeons that also mentions virgin spirits, and this passage (Nag Hammadi Codex III:88–89, cited in the commentary) is very close to the text under consideration. Cf. also Wisdom of Jesus Christ (Nag Hammadi Codex III), 113; On the Origin of the World, 105–6.

[106] These aeons and luminaries, the spiritual powers of the universe, represent aspects of the world, especially time and units of time. On the twelve aeons, compare the months of the year or the signs of the zodiac. On the seventy-two heavens and luminaries, compare the traditional number of nations in the world, according to Jewish lore. On the three hundred sixty firmaments, compare the number of days in the solar year (thirty days per month, for twelve months), without five intercalary days. This passage in the Gospel of Judas is paralleled in Eugnostos the Blessed III:83–84 (cited in the commentary), and in the lines that follow in Eugnostos the Blessed, the author discusses a similar number of aeons, heavens, and firmaments.

that is, perdition[107]—by the Father and the seventy-two luminaries who are with the Self-Generated and his seventy-two aeons. In him[108] the first human appeared with his incorruptible powers. And the aeon that appeared with his generation, the aeon in whom are the cloud of knowledge[109] and the angel, is called [51] El.[110] [...] aeon [...] after that [...] said, 'Let twelve angels come into being [to] rule over chaos and the [underworld].' And look, from the cloud there appeared an [angel] whose face flashed with fire and whose appearance was defiled with blood. His name was Nebro,[111] which means 'rebel';[112] others call him Yaldabaoth.[113] Another angel, Saklas,[114] also came from

---

[107] Our cosmos, unlike the divine realm above, is susceptible to decay and hence may be termed a realm of perdition.

[108] Or, "In it"—that is, in the cosmos.

[109] Coptic, from Greek, *gnōsis*.

[110] El is an ancient Semitic name for God. In Sethian texts, related names, such as Eloaios, are used for powers and authorities of this world. The Secret Book of John also refers to Elohim, the Hebrew word for "God" in the Jewish Scriptures.

[111] In Holy Book of the Great Invisible Spirit III:57, Nebruel is a great demoness who mates with Saklas and produces twelve aeons; cf. also the role of Nebroel in Manichaean texts. Here the name Nebro is given without the honorific suffix -el (also "God" in Hebrew; cf. the name El, above). In Secret Book of John II:10, the demiurge Yaldabaoth has the appearance of a snake with the face of a lion, and his eyes are like flashing bolts of lightning. In Holy Book of the Great Invisible Spirit III:56–57, Sophia of matter is bloody in appearance: "A cloud [named] Sophia of matter appeared .... [She] surveyed the regions [of chaos], and her face looked like ... in her appearance ... blood."

[112] Or, "apostate" (Coptic, from Greek, *apostatēs*). Nebro most likely derives from Nebrod in Genesis 10:8–12 (cf. 1 Chronicles 1:10) of the Septuagint, where Nebrod (Hebrew Nimrod) reflects the tradition of a well-known legendary figure in the ancient Middle East. The word Nimrod may be related to the Hebrew word for "rebel."

[113] Yaldabaoth is a common name for the demiurge in Sethian texts. Yaldabaoth probably means "child of chaos" (or, less likely, "child of (S)abaoth") in Aramaic.

[114] Saklas (or Sakla, as in Gospel of Judas 52) is another common name for the demiurge in Sethian texts. *Saklas* (or *Sakla*) means "fool" in Aramaic.

the cloud. So Nebro created six angels—as well as Saklas—to be assistants, and these produced twelve angels in the heavens, with each one receiving a portion in the heavens.[115]

THE RULERS AND ANGELS

"The twelve rulers spoke with the twelve angels: 'Let each of you [52] [...] and let them [...] generation [—*one line lost*—] angels':

The first is [S]eth, who is called Christ.[116]
The [second] is Harmathoth, who is [...].
The [third] is Galila.
The fourth is Yobel.
The fifth [is] Adonaios.

---

[115] The syntax of this sentence is not entirely clear, so that the role of Saklas and his relationship with Nebro remain uncertain. If Nebro and Saklas each create six angels, that accounts for the twelve angels that are produced. Cf. Holy Book of the Great Invisible Spirit III:57–58: "Sakla the great [angel observed] Nebruel the great demon who is with him. [Together] they brought a spirit of reproduction to the earth, and [they produced] angelic assistants. Sakla [said] to Nebruel the great [demon], 'Let twelve realms come into being in the ... realm, worlds ....' Through the will of the Self-Generated, [Sakla] the great angel said, 'There shall be ... seven in number ....'"

[116] Here, as in other Christian Sethian texts, Christ is described as the manifestation of Seth in this world. In Holy Book of the Great Invisible Spirit III:63–64, the text refers to "the incorruptible one, conceived by the Word [*Logos*], the living Jesus, with whom great Seth has been clothed." In Three Forms of First Thought 50, the Word, or Logos, declares, "I put on Jesus. I carried him from the accursed wood [the cross] and established him in the dwelling places of his Father." Cf. Gospel of Judas 56.

These are the five who ruled over the underworld, and first of all over chaos.[117]

THE CREATION OF HUMANITY

"Then Saklas said to his angels, 'Let us create a human being after the likeness and after the image.'[118] They fashioned Adam and his wife Eve, who is called, in the cloud, Zoe.[119] For by this name all the generations seek the man, and each of them calls the woman by these names. Now, Sakla did not [53] com[mand ...] except [...] the gene[rations ...] this [...]. And the [ruler] said to Adam, 'You shall live long, with your children.'"[120]

---

[117] In Holy Book of the Great Invisible Spirit III:58, through Nebruel and Sakla twelve angels are produced, several of which have names similar or identical to the names here, and mention is made of Cain (this passage is quoted in the commentary of this book). The reference to Cain may bring to mind the claim of Irenaeus of Lyon (*Against Heresies* 1.31.1) that the people who composed the Gospel of Judas appealed to the authority of Cain, though Cain is not mentioned in the extant text of the Gospel of Judas. In Secret Book of John II:10–11, a similar list of names is given, and it is said that seven rule over the seven spheres of heaven (those of the sun, moon, and five planets then known—Mercury, Venus, Mars, Jupiter, and Saturn) and five rule over the depth of the abyss.

[118] Cf. Genesis 1:26. Similar accounts of the creation of a human being are found in other Sethian texts, and sometimes it is said, in more fully developed traditions, that the human is created after the image of God above and with a likeness to the rulers of this world. Cf. Secret Book of John II:15, cited in the commentary of this book.

[119] Zoe, Greek for "life," is the name of Eve in the Septuagint.

[120] Cf. Genesis 1:28, 5:3–5. The demiurge seems true to his word: The people described in the early chapters of Genesis are said to have lived extraordinarily long lives.

Judas Asks About the Destiny
of Adam and Humanity

Judas said to Jesus, "[What] is the long duration of time that the human being will live?"

Jesus said, "Why are you wondering about this, that Adam, with his generation, has lived his span of life in the place where he has received his kingdom, with longevity with his ruler?"[121]

Judas said to Jesus, "Does the human spirit die?"

Jesus said, "This is why God ordered Michael to give the spirits of people to them as a loan, so that they might offer service, but the Great One ordered Gabriel[122] to grant spirits to the great generation with no ruler over it[123]—that is, the spirit and the soul.[124]

---

[121] This sentence is difficult and the translation tentative, but it seems to mean that Judas is wondering about Adam in his world with his length of life and his god—all of which is irrelevant for Judas. At the end, the sentence reads, literally, "in a number with his ruler?"

[122] Michael and Gabriel are two prominent archangels.

[123] Or, "the kingless generation," a reference to the generation of Seth, using a description familiar from Sethian texts to indicate that the people of Seth are indomitable.

[124] God, apparently the god of this world, gives the spirit of life (the breath of life? Perhaps cf. Genesis 2:7) to people, through Michael, as a loan, but the Great Spirit gives spirit and soul to people, through Gabriel, as a gift. Genesis 2:7 can be interpreted creatively in other gnostic texts, including Sethian texts; cf. Secret Book of John II:19: "They [five luminaries from above] said to Yaldabaoth, 'Breathe some of your spirit into the face of Adam, and the body will arise.' He breathed his spirit into Adam. The spirit is the power of his mother [Sophia], but he did not realize this, because he lives in ignorance. The Mother's power went out of Yaldabaoth and into the psychical body that had been made to be like the one who is from the beginning. The body moved, and became powerful. And it was enlightened." On spirit and soul in the present text, cf. also Gospel of Judas 43.

Therefore, the [rest] of the souls [54] [—*one line missing*—].[125]

JESUS DISCUSSES THE DESTRUCTION OF THE WICKED WITH JUDAS AND OTHERS

"[…] light [—*nearly two lines missing*—] around […] let […] spirit [that is] within you[126] dwell in this [flesh] among the generations of angels. But God caused knowledge[127] to be [given] to Adam and those with him,[128] so that the kings of chaos and the underworld might not lord it over them."

Judas said to Jesus, "So what will those generations do?"

Jesus said, "Truly[129] I say to you,[130] for all of them the stars bring matters to completion.[131] When Saklas completes the span of time assigned for him, their first

---

[125] Here the Coptic reads, in part, *toou*, which means "mountain"; it may also be restored to read {*ᵉn}toou*, "they." In the following fragmentary section, second-person plural pronominal forms appear, and this seems to indicate that Jesus is in the company of more people than only Judas. Probably the other disciples are also included in this discussion.

[126] Plural.

[127] Again, Coptic, from Greek, *gnōsis*.

[128] This passage suggests that *gnōsis*, or knowledge, is given to Adam and thus to humanity. The way in which Adam and humanity come to possess knowledge is explained in detail in other gnostic texts, including Sethian texts, and in these texts it is asserted that humanity has knowledge but the megalomaniacal rulers of this world do not.

[129] Here and in subsequent text, the Coptic word *alēthōs* (from Greek) is used rather than *hamēn*, as earlier in the text.

[130] Plural.

[131] The references to the stars, their influences, and their eventual destruction are astronomical and apocalyptic.

star will appear with the generations, and they will finish what they said they would do. Then they will fornicate in my name and slay their children[132] [55] and they will [...] and [—*about six and a half lines missing*—] my name, and he will [...] your star over the [thir]teenth aeon."

After that Jesus [laughed].

[Judas said], "Master, [why are you laughing at us]?"[133]

[Jesus] answered [and said], "I am not laughing [at you] but at the error of the stars, because these six stars wander about with these five combatants, and they all will be destroyed along with their creatures."[134]

JESUS SPEAKS OF THOSE WHO ARE BAPTIZED, AND JUDAS'S BETRAYAL

Judas said to Jesus, "Look, what will those who have been baptized in your name do?"[135]

Jesus said, "Truly I say [to you], this baptism [56]

---

[132] Cf. Ezekiel 16:15–22, as well as Gospel of Judas 38 and 40, on slaying children and committing fornication.

[133] The restoration is tentative.

[134] The wandering stars are probably the five planets (Mercury, Venus, Mars, Jupiter, and Saturn) along with the moon. According to ancient astronomical and astrological theory, such wandering stars can rule over us and influence our lives in unpleasant ways. Cf. also Gospel of Judas 37.

[135] These are Christians baptized in the name of Christ. Whether this is meant as a criticism of ordinary Christian baptism, as in other Sethian texts, is unclear.

[...] my name [—*about nine lines missing*—] to me. Truly [I] say to you, Judas, [those who] offer sacrifices to Saklas[136] [...] God [—*three lines missing*—] everything that is evil.

"But you will exceed all of them. For you will sacrifice the man that clothes me.[137]

Already your horn has been raised,
your wrath has been kindled,
your star has shown brightly,
and your heart has {...}.[138] [57]

"Truly [...][139] your last [...] become [—*about two and a half lines missing*—], since he will be destroyed. And then the image[140] of the great generation of Adam will be exalted, for prior to heaven, earth, and the angels, that generation, which is from the eternal realms, exists.[141] Look, you have been told everything.

---

[136] On offering sacrifices to Saklas, perhaps cf. Gospel of Judas 38–41.

[137] Literally, "that bears me" (Coptic, from Greek, *etrphorei* *ᵉmmoei*). Judas is instructed by Jesus to help him by sacrificing the fleshly body ("the man") that clothes or bears the true spiritual self of Jesus. The death of Jesus, with the assistance of Judas, is taken to be the liberation of the spiritual person within.

[138] On the poetic lines depicting how Judas is prepared for his act of salvific betrayal, cf. passages from the Psalms. The last line may be restored to read "[become strong]," or the like.

[139] Perhaps restore to read "Truly [I say ...]," or the like.

[140] Coptic, from Greek, *tupos*. The text, restored to read *(tu)pos,* may also be restored as [*to*]*pos,* "place" (also from Greek).

[141] That is, the generation of Seth is a preexistent generation that comes from God.

Lift up your eyes and look at the cloud and the light within it and the stars surrounding it. The star that leads the way is your star."[142]

Judas lifted up his eyes and saw the luminous cloud, and he entered it.[143] Those standing on the ground[144] heard a voice coming from the cloud, saying, [58] [...] great generation [...] ... image [...] [—*about five lines missing*—].[145]

CONCLUSION: JUDAS BETRAYS JESUS

[...] Their high priests murmured because [he][146] had gone into the guest room[147] for his prayer.[148] But some scribes were there watching carefully in order to arrest him during the prayer, for they were afraid of the people, since he was regarded by all as a prophet.[149]

---

[142] Judas is literally the star of the text.

[143] This passage may be described as the transfiguration of Judas. He is vindicated by being glorified in the luminous cloud, and a voice speaks from the cloud. As in accounts of the transfiguration of Jesus (Matthew 17:1–8, Mark 9:2–8, Luke 9:28–36; cf. Book of Allogenes 61–62, just after the Gospel of Judas in Codex Tchacos), here Judas enters a luminous cloud, on high, and a divine voice speaks.

[144] Or, "below."

[145] Most of the words of the divine voice from the cloud are lost in the lacuna in the manuscript, but it may have praised Judas and the great generation or offered conclusions about the meaning of the events described. On a divine voice in the New Testament gospels, compare the accounts of the transfiguration of Jesus as well as the baptism of Jesus (Matthew 3:13–17; Mark 1:9–11; Luke 3:21–22).

[146] Jesus. The restoration "[they]"—that is, Jesus and the disciples—is also possible.

[147] Coptic, from Greek, *kataluma*. The same word is used in Mark 14:14 and Luke 22:11 for the guest room where the Last Supper was celebrated.

[148] This clause may also be translated as direct speech: "Their high priests murmured, '[He] has (or [They] have) gone into the guest room for his prayer.'"

[149] Cf. Matthew 26:1–5; Mark 14:1–2; Luke 22:1–2; John 11:45–53.

They approached Judas and said to him, "What are you doing here? You are Jesus' disciple."

Judas answered them as they wished. And he received some money and handed him over to them.[150]

THE GOSPEL OF JUDAS[151]

---

[150] Cf. Matthew 26:14–16, 44–56; Mark 14:10–11, 41–50; Luke 22:3–6, 45–53; John 18:1–11. The conclusion of the Gospel of Judas is presented in subtle and understated terms, and there is no account of the actual crucifixion of Jesus.

[151] Here the wording of the titular subscript is not "The Gospel According to [*pkata* or *kata*] Judas," as is the case in most gospel texts, but "The Gospel of [^{e}n-] Judas." It is possible that the title means to suggest that this is the gospel, or good news, about Judas and the place of Judas in the tradition. What he accomplished, the text concludes, is not bad news but good news for Judas and for all who would come after Judas—and Jesus.

The Story of Codex Tchacos
and the Gospel of Judas

Rodolphe Kasser

I let out a cry when I saw for the first time, on the evening of July 24, 2001, "the object" my very embarrassed visitors had brought for me to examine. It was still a completely unknown cultural document at this date, with such a powerful text and yet written on material so frail, so sickly in appearance, so close to ultimate extinction. The papyrus codex written in Coptic, more than sixteen hundred years old, had been damaged by so many misfortunes, many of which could have been avoided. It was a stark victim of cupidity and ambition. My cry was provoked by the striking vision of the object so precious but so badly mistreated, broken up to the extreme, partially pulverized, infinitely fragile, crumbling at the least contact; the "ancient book," to which was later to be given the name "Codex Tchacos," was that evening a poor small thing pitifully packed at the bottom of a cardboard box.

How was it possible that such vandalism could occur at the dawn of the twenty-first century? How could this have happened in a milieu—one of art merchants—well known for the gentleness of its methods and careful work? Or worse yet, in an environment even more noble and honorable, the world of scholarship?

July 24, 2001, clearly divides the history of Codex Tchacos into a "before" and "after" phase. After this date, I can tell of my own experiences. But concerning what really happened to the Codex pages before this date, I have no personal knowledge. However, the codex bears the scars of this period.

The Maecenas Foundation for Ancient Art, the current owner of the codex, which has the responsibility for safeguarding it and providing the initial publication of its content, has made a considerable effort in trying to reconstruct the "before" phase and asked Herb Krosney to investigate and document this search independently. His zealous efforts are provided in his book, *The Lost Gospel* (National Geographic Society, 2006), and I have had the opportunity to take note of some of his findings.

In its present dilapidated state, Codex Tchacos contains

parts of thirty-three folios, or sixty-six pages, paginated regularly in the numbers that survive (because of the mutilation of the folios, the numbers for pages 5, 31–32, and 49–66 have disappeared). This manuscript is sometimes called "Codex of Judas," from the name of one of its texts, but it contains in fact four different tractates:

- pages 1–9, the Letter of Peter to Philip (with approximately the same text as the second tractate of Codex VIII of the Nag Hammadi library, with the same title);
- pages 10–32, "James" (with approximately the same text as the third tractate of Codex V of the Nag Hammadi library, there entitled the Revelation of James or the First Revelation of James);
- pages 33–58, the Gospel of Judas (a completely unknown text until now, though its title was mentioned by Irenaeus in his work *Against Heresies*);
- pages 59–66, a seriously damaged tractate, to the point that its title has been lost, but which scholars have agreed to designate the Book of Allogenes, from the name of the main character in the tractate (this tractate has no connection with the third

tractate of Nag Hammadi Codex XI, entitled Allogenes, or Allogenes the Stranger).

Dark Birth Followed by a Tormented
Childhood: The Egyptian and Greek Dealings

Herb Krosney reports that the codex was found during
a clandestine outing, probably around 1978, in Middle
Egypt. The linguistic patterns found in the texts of this
manuscript confirm this origin, since all of them belong
to a local Middle Egyptian variety of Sahidic (the southern supralocal Coptic dialect). The excavator probed a
tomb dug in the side of the Jebel Qarara (right bank) of
the Nile River, dominating the village of Ambar close
to Maghagha, sixty kilometers north of Al Minya.

Antiquities dealers, whose role proved to be considerable in this business, were contacted after this discovery. One was an Egyptian named Hanna, who lived in
Heliopolis, a suburb northeast of Cairo. Hanna didn't
know any language other than Arabic, and had gained
possession of the codex through a colleague in Middle
Egypt. Am Samiah (a pseudonym), a friend of the dis-
coverers of the codex, sold it to Hanna, on whom the
papyrus document made a very strong impression.

Hanna had assembled a host of precious items in his

Cairo apartment to display to a new customer, but, before the customer returned to pay for the objects, Hanna found his apartment emptied by nighttime robbers. The major pieces stolen were the codex, a gold statuette of Isis, and a gold necklace. In subsequent years, objects that had been stolen from Hanna started to pop up in Europe. He decided to travel to Geneva and talk to a Greek dealer who had been regularly buying from him, to seek assistance in retrieving the stolen items. In 1982, with the Greek dealer's help, Hanna eventually succeeded in recovering the codex.

Even before the theft, Hanna had consulted several experts, probably European papyrologists, to determine how valuable the codex was, and their response prompted him to seek an extremely high selling price. We don't know exactly who gave that incautious and questionable valuation.

Immediately after its recovery, Hanna tried by all means available to him to sell his manuscript, looking for an institution endowed with sufficient financial means to meet the price he had put on his treasure. It certainly was an exalted enterprise, but one in which he was out of his depth. Eventually, Hanna succeeded in contacting Ludwig Koenen, a member of the Department of Classical Studies of the University of Michigan.

The fifty-two Coptic gnostic or gnosticizing treatises

discovered in 1945 near Nag Hammadi in Upper Egypt, identified for the first time by Jean Doresse, had caused an exceptional interest at that time among Coptologists, historians of religion, and theologians. Between 1970 and 1980, this interest was close to its apogee. European along with American Coptologists and gnostic scholars were concluding their various contributions of research and publication in this area, and one of the leaders in this enterprise was James M. Robinson, who had helped conduct the research on Coptic gnostic manuscripts of Nag Hammadi. These scholars closely followed the European and American markets of antiquities in the hope of being able to recover (and find some sponsor or university to buy) one or another of the folios currently lost among the thirteen codices of the Nag Hammadi library or more or less similar texts to those that had already been discovered and identified.

Failure at Geneva

Hanna's intriguing offer led to Koenen contacting Robinson. Koenen told him that he would go to Geneva in May 1983 to negotiate the purchase of three papyrus codices. The first, the only one that interested him, included a Greek mathematical text. The second, in

Greek also, was a book of the Old Testament, and it interested one of his colleagues, David Noel Freedman, who would accompany him in Geneva. The third codex, containing only Coptic, didn't interest the others, but they supposed that it would interest Robinson. He was thus offered the opportunity to participate in these negotiations, while also contributing to the search for the funds needed to make the purchase. The Californian's answer was affirmative. Unable to go himself, Robinson sent in his place Stephen Emmel, one of his best students, along with $50,000 for the intended purchase.

That sum, along with the additional moneys available to Koenen and Freedman, was certainly substantial, but it was not even close to the amount required by Hanna for his "three" manuscripts. In fact, the third, the one in Coptic, was composed of two distinct codices, the codex of Judas's gospel and a codex containing letters of Paul; had Hanna known this, he might have used the pretext to increase his price. Even so, an abyss separated money the scholars offered and Hanna's demand, and very quickly the negotiations broke down. He believed the texts were equal in worth to those found at Nag Hammadi. Since the media attention focused a quarter century before on the texts of Nag Hammadi had put them nearly on the same level of the famous Dead Sea Scrolls, the uproar had turned his head. The purchase was not consummated, and the three potential purchasers went back home, their hands empty.

In this case, the enterprise quickly ended in failure, because of the extraordinary price of the seller and the fact that the researchers had not been able to do anything more than glimpse discreetly the coveted text for a scant hour. Afterward, it would disappear for long years in a dark bank vault, and was in danger of vanishing completely, if some physical accident, during its ill-advised journeys, reduced it to dust or ashes.

Here intrudes the question of scientific morals, or deontology (any consideration of individual friendship or antipathy being put aside). A temporary lapse can be forgiven, accepting that one believes a private purchase to be a more efficient process, if it is recognized later that the chosen option had not been beneficial scientifically. The best ethical choice for the codex would have been to alert, giving them all necessary information to act, other Coptologists, gnostic scholars, even if they belonged to some "rival" side. Combined, the competing teams could have possibly located more considerable financial support, and so they would have been able to "catch the big fish." As it turns out, a few notes, in several academic publications, signaled the existence of a new gnostic witness, however in an elliptical fashion, not permitting anyone the depth of knowledge needed to approach the antiquarian possessor of the document and secure it for the researchers concerned. Some of these more precise details probably circulated "between friends," but without going beyond the confines of a very personal and confidential setting. "Cooperative deontology," if such an expression may be used, might have rescued the manuscript far earlier. Instead, scholars had to fly from the United States to Switzerland to buy a treasure that neither Swiss nor other European Coptologists had any idea existed.

At the time, the Maecenas Foundation had not yet been created, beginning only in 1994. Yet in 1982, Frieda Tchacos Nussberger, herself born in Egypt and now living in Zurich as a dealer in ancient art, had followed Hanna and his attempts to sell the codex. She received a photo of a "page 5/19" of the codex. This odd numbering for the folio came about because, already between its discovery and 1982, the energetic handling to which the manuscript had been submitted had produced a more or less horizontal deep fold, apparently affecting all of the folios, and each of them had separated into an upper fragment (about a third or a quarter of the folio) and a lower fragment (the remaining two-thirds or three-quarters of the folio). The upper fragment carried the pagination, which permitted me later to situate without hesitation the upper fragments in relation to the others, but this advantage was denied the lower fragments. In nearly all cases, a crumbling of one to two centimeters had gnawed away the folded portion, widening the gap; this prevented direct contact between the upper and lower fragments and produced a series of small fragments only millimeters in size, making it nearly impossible to identify and to fit the adjoining fragment to the one corresponding to it. The numbering in the photo of 1982 was 5/19, because whoever arranged the fragments for the photograph, mistakenly or deliberately, placed the top of page 5 with the bottom of page 19; twenty years later, as a consequence of these manipulations, the Coptologists beginning to decipher the texts of the codex had in front of them several other photos of crossed fragments, 5/13, 13/21, and so forth.

Stephen Emmel wrote a report after the 1983 inspection that reveals the respect with which he handled the papyrus text. Following the orders given by the owner, he avoided manipulating it. His report shows his obvious concern to protect to the utmost extent possible the physical structure of the codex:

> The leaves and fragments of the codex will need to be conserved between panes of glass. I would recommend conservation measures patterned after those used to restore and conserve the Nag

Hammadi codices.... Despite the breakage that has already occurred, and that which will inevitably occur between now and the proper conservation of the manuscript, I estimate that it would require about a month to reassemble the fragments of the manuscript.

After having reviewed the codex for a second time twenty-two years later—after it had been recovered, in an imperiled state, by the Foundation—he testified that to his memory, in 1983 the fragmentation was relatively little advanced. This is how his earlier report described it:

Certainly the gem of the entire collection of four manuscripts is item 2, a papyrus codex from the 4th century A.D., approximately 30 cm tall and 15 cm broad, containing gnostic texts. At the time that the codex was discovered, it was probably in good condition, with a leather binding and complete leaves with all four margins intact. But the codex has been badly handled.

It had been "badly handled" already, between the moment of its discovery and that inspection on May 15, 1983, and its condition would worsen seriously between then and 2005. He continued:

Only half of the leather binding (probably the front cover) is now preserved and the leaves have suffered some breakage. The absence of half of the binding and the fact that page numbers run only into the 50's lead me to suppose that the back half of the codex may be missing; only closer study can prove or disprove this supposition. The texts are in a non-standard form of Sahidic.... The codex contains at least three different texts: (1) "The First Apocalypse of James" known already, though in a different version, from Nag Hammadi Codex (NHC) V; (2) "The Letter of Peter to Philip" known already from NHC VIII ... ; and (3) a dialogue between Jesus and his disciples (at least "Judas" [i.e., presumably, Judas Thomas] is involved) similar in genre to "The Dialogue of the Savior" (NHC III) and "The Wisdom of Jesus Christ" (NHC III and the Berlin gnostic codex [PB 8502]).

As it turns out, "items" 1 and 2 were correctly identified (although in an incorrect order), but Emmel misunderstood who Judas was in item 3. In an article in 2005 *(Watani International)*, Robinson suggests an explanation: "The seller had forbidden his visitors to write any notes or take any photographs, but Emmel had evaded the edict surreptitiously. He excused himself to go to the bathroom, where he transcribed what his acute eye and memory had retained of the Coptic material. He afterward wrote up his notes in a confidential memorandum."

The episode makes one wonder what would have

happened had Emmel, by some stratagem, been able, for several minutes at least, to investigate the codex in its owner's absence, even to photograph some characteristic passages of it. A more in-depth perusal would have likely suggested an overhaul of the report, taking into account information that he didn't possess in June 1983. Such additional information would have corrected the "mistake" on the exact title of "James" (*Iakkōbos,* not Secret Book of James) and the position of the small treatise entitled the Letter of Peter to Philip, which, the pagination proves, precedes "James" in the codex.

Between 1983 and 2001: Further and Accelerated Destruction

We have little precise information about what happened to the papyri during the seventeen years that elapsed between May 15, 1983, and April 3, 2000, the date on which Frieda Tchacos Nussberger for the first time obtained possession of the codex. Through documentary evidence at the Maecenas Foundation, we know now that, on March 23, 1984, Hanna rented a safe-deposit box with Citibank in a Hicksville, New York, branch and that he kept this safe-deposit box until April 3, 2000, the date on which he sold his manuscripts to Frieda Nussberger. The inquiry conducted by Herb Krosney has shown that some-time in 1984 Hanna contacted New York manuscript dealer Hans P. Kraus, as well as Professor Roger Bagnall from Columbia University in New York, offering his man-uscripts for sale. We may assume that during the subse-quent years Hanna eventually understood that his asking price was too high and that he would never succeed in sell-ing his objects at that value. The manuscripts remained all through these years enclosed in the narrow box suffering from the frequently changing but generally humid cli-mate of this New York suburb.

On April 3, 2000, Nussberger deposited the codex for some months, for examination, in the Beinecke Library at Yale University. While there, specialists had access to it, to probe it a little in order to know its con-tents better. During its stay at the Beinecke Library, Bentley Layton succeeded in identifying the third trea-tise contained in the codex as the Gospel of Judas (Iscariot). Nevertheless, in August 2000, Yale made known that it was not going to purchase the codex.

On September 9, 2000, Nussberger sold the object to an American antiquarian named Bruce Ferrini, who is said to have frozen it, a process that lessened its integrity in a catastrophic manner. After a calamitous sojourn in the moistness of numerous American summers, this inauspi-cious freezing apparently produced the partial destruction of the sap holding the fibers of the papyrus together, making it significantly more fragile—and susceptible to crumbling, producing the weakest folios of papyrus that professional papyrologists had ever seen, a fragility that is a true nightmare for the restorer. Furthermore, this freezing made all the water in the fibers migrate toward the surface of the papyrus before evaporation, bringing with it quantities of pigment from inside the fibers, which darkened many pages of the papyrus and therefore made the writing extremely difficult to read.

Unable to fulfill his financial obligations to Frieda Nussberger, the antiquarian committed to return the totality of the parts of the codex in his possession, along with any transcriptions and all photos he had taken. However, later events indicated that Ferrini, after delivering the materials to Nussberger, still had several fragments of pages, at least some of which he sold elsewhere. In addition, he had many photographs of pages, providing them to the Coptologist Charles W. Hedrick.

At this point, the Swiss lawyer who had been helping Frieda Nussberger to recover her manuscripts from Ferrini suggested an acquisition of the codex by his Maecenas Foundation for Ancient Art, in Basel. Nussberger accepted his offer on the spot, and the codex was officially imported to Switzerland on February 19, 2001, in the name of the Foundation.

Consonant with its objectives, the Foundation wanted to have the codex withdrawn from the notable risks of circulating in the market; professionally restored, conserved, and published; and eventually donated to an appropriate institution in Egypt, its country of origin. Egyptian authorities have since accepted the promised donation and have designated the Coptic Museum of Cairo as the final home of the codex. These are the circumstances that led up to the meeting of July 24, 2001.

Miraculous Resurrection: Diagnosis and First Measures

At the beginning of July 2001, destiny (if such terminology is allowed) appeared unexpectedly, setting in motion the process that was going to transform the "despaired case" of Codex Tchacos—close to extinction after a long period of agony—to a "case full of hope," in spite of the damage undergone, of which some had unfortunately become irreversible. The case promised to have a glorious future, as Stephen Emmel had mentioned in his report of June 1, 1983: "I strongly urge you to acquire this gnostic codex. It is of the utmost scholarly worth, comparable in every way to any one of the Nag Hammadi codices."

As a result from successive astonishing coincidences, I was called by the Maecenas Foundation. A meeting followed, in Zurich on the twenty-fourth of the month. What I had been told about the papyrus codex in question excited my curiosity, and I asked permission to see it first. I added the following proposition: If the examination of the enigmatic object proved to be positive, I could possibly advise Maecenas about the best procedures to take. If the texts written on the papyrus were sufficiently interesting, I proposed to prepare them for publication. The manuscript had to be restored meticulously and consolidated. This would not be a small business if—given the most pessimistic hypothesis—its status was considered close to total disintegration. Then every folio of the codex would be put under glass, in order to be photographed, since an essential part of the preparation of the edition would be made on the basis of excellent photographs, in order to handle the original the least amount possible. Still, it was an enticing project, stimulating, one creating enthusiasm while retaining strict standards. At the end of this process, Maecenas, in accordance with its principles, would give back to Egypt a manuscript worthy of its ancient civilization, an object provided with all the care it could need, completely restored, correctly published. This process could be considered a model of collaboration between Maecenas and the injured nation.

It would be unjust to pass over the enormous debt of recognition that the scientific community owes Maecenas for its restoration of the papyrus, the progressive photographic work, and the establishment of the conditions making possible the edition of the texts contained in the codex. If this previously luckless manuscript is resuscitated today from the black hole to which it seemed destined, with its cultural wealth completely unknown up to now, this miracle—the term is not exaggerated—Coptic scholars and theologians owe to Maecenas's exemplary perseverance in this remarkable operation.

Let us return to a narration of the events of July 24, 2001. I first saw the famous codex that evening. I expected a surprise, and it certainly it was. When they showed it to me, it was huddled up at the bottom of a cardboard box—the remains of what had been a pristine papyrus codex, maybe of the first half of the fourth century. What I could see from this initial perusal of the text showed it was written in a Sahidic supralocal dialect of the Coptic language, crossed with dialectical influences evoking some local dialect of Middle Egypt. That corresponded with what I was told about the place of the discovery: the region of Al Minya. This first glance, appeasing my curiosity, was for me an electrifying experience, inviting me to guess what lay in the secret garden of the text. Sweet rapture, yes, deeply stimulating, but one followed by a brutal shock. During my long career, I have had before my eyes many Coptic or Greek documents on papyrus, sometimes very "sick," but damaged to this point, never! In many places, the papyrus was so blackened that reading had become practically impossible. The papyrus had become so weakened that it didn't tolerate the least touching; nearly all contact, as light as it was, threatened to leave it in dust. It was a case apparently without hope.

However, after the first shock, the codex's attraction became irresistible when I found one of its colophons, placed in such a way that it seemed to be on its final page, announcing a treatise considered irreparably lost: *peuaggelion nioudas*, the Gospel of Judas. This justified at least an introductory probe. And while valuing the success of the enterprise, all didn't appear hopelessly negative. Huddled up in the box that contained it, with its fragile and broken-up folios, the codex appeared to have escaped a piecemeal scattering. Even if most of the middle part of the folios had been broken in about ten fragments, at least I could reasonably believe that they had remained concentrated in the box. By taking them out carefully, with as little disturbance as possible, then restoring, consolidating them somewhat, I would perhaps succeed, with a great deal of patience and luck as well, in pasting them together again, thus reconstituting some parts of the dismembered folios. Another reason for moderate optimism was that the upper margin of the pages seemed rather little damaged, meaning there was the possibility of continuous pagination. That would permit me to establish successive folios, containing words never found in this ancient condition, belonging to an entirely new gospel. The owners of the codex accepted this preliminary verdict and offered quite generously to take care of the initial expenses.

The first necessary measure to take without delay in the restoration was setting under glass, one by one, all of the folios, including the incomplete fragments. Important parts of the binding of the codex were missing, and, apart from a few sections in the center, its folios were no longer fixed to each other. After protecting the folios this way, we could then adjust them more freely, with lower risk, photograph the pages, and finally read the text progressively, while aiming to translate the whole. This meticulous work was undertaken immediately. I need to emphasize here the expertise and dexterity that was put into this operation of incomparable difficulty and gentleness by Florence Darbre, the director of the Atelier de Restauration (Nyon), which was commissioned in this work. With her fairy's fingers, she made largely possible what, at first glance, appeared doomed to failure.

Instrumental also in our success in establishing, transcribing, translating, and commenting on the revealed text was the excellent professional work, at every step of the way, provided by photographer Christian Poite of Geneva. The quality of the pictures he obtained was an inestimable help in our struggle to identify the severely damaged letters, too often blurry because of the disastrous condition of the papyrus. Thus, the work, conducted with exactitude and tenacity, soon bore its first fruits.

Then, in 2004, I proceeded to obtain the services of an excellent collaborator in the person of Gregor Wurst, a Coptologist in his own right. Thanks to the unusually delicate work of restoration, to our investigation and assessment, it became possible to confirm what previous observers from before 2001 had been able to only glimpse, that this codex contained four successive texts. The fourth (designated the Book of Allogenes) appeared to my collaborator, Gregor Wurst, and to myself only during the year 2004. We already had received indications of its existence: An important leftover from the pagination of the codex was kept, and this preliminary observation first raised high hopes, since the number of the folios relatively well kept seemed to reach and even pass a little the figure of thirty. These hopes, however, soon would prove to be cruelly disappointed.

Indeed, as the examination of the document became

more and more advanced, it became apparent that our codex, before its acquisition by Maecenas, had undergone, presumably on behalf of some of the antiquarians that had it in their possession, various imprudent, careless manipulations that often led our scientific research into error.

RESTORATION AND RECOMPOSITION

Codex Tchacos had submitted to the pressure of a hand more impatient than respectful of the fragility of the object. It is not hard to imagine a ravenous eye, greedy to see more of the text inside the hardly penetrable mass formed by the compact heap of the superimposed pieces of papyrus. All the folios of the manuscript had, alas, been broken brutally at (about) two-thirds of their height by the deep fold previously mentioned. This rupture had divided every page into two parts of unequal area. The upper fragments have the pagination and very little text. The lower fragments are evidently devoid of pagination, but their advantage is their relative wealth of coherent text. However, the violence to the whole has made it especially difficult to identify and set in the correct position the majority of the lower fragments, having lost all reliable contact with the corresponding upper portions, and with the lower fragments having been mixed up by an ill-advised hand.

What? I wondered. The codex had been abused, reshuffled, robbed, by whom? For what reason? It seemed completely unlikely and scandalous to imagine scientific researchers mistreating, in contempt of all ethical considerations, the manuscript before conducting its restoration, solely in their inconsiderate hurry to know, before hypothetical competitors, the content of these texts still unknown.

A merchant of antiquities, on the contrary, may have other priorities and interests. Certainly, he doesn't want to risk too much damage (or to allow damage by an auxiliary photographer) to the object he expects will fetch a good price. But "one doesn't make an omelette without breaking an egg," and he will have difficulty convincing a potential purchaser (especially if the required price is very high) if he cannot display photos of some parts of the text (colophons and other titles, decorated in a suggestive manner), exciting the buyer's curiosity. Even if it may happen that a researcher does lend his participation to such an operation, few would dare risk damage to the manuscript in the hope of increasing the price before a time could be planned for a wise and methodical exploration of the manuscript. The correction of this cavalier intrusion in the first half of the codex was made by the analysis of the upper and lower fragments containing the Letter of Peter to Philip and "James," for which we have, in the collection of Nag Hammadi, enough parallel texts to permit identification of the matching lower pieces. Unfortunately, the order of the Gospel of Judas's lower sections (without any parallel text available) remained much less sure. It could be determined with certainty only by the quality of the fibers of the papyrus, although more rarely we could use the negative narrative argument, when the beginning of the text of the lower fragment could absolutely not be the continuation of the text of the upper portion.

All indications give the impression that the codex may have been shuffled about to optimize its commercial appeal—complicating to the extreme the task of the investigator. It seemed to have been reorganized quite extensively, perhaps to make it superficially more attractive, thus sharpening the curiosity of a potential customer.

In a satisfying manner, the "packet" of about thirty folios appeared to conclude with the final title—titles then normally appearing at the end—"Gospel of Judas." Symmetrically, it might have seemed appropriate to present a "pretty title" in the beginning of the packet as well, which could explain why the end of the Letter of Peter bearing the title, actually the lower part of page 9, came to be placed below the upper portion of page 1, the beginning of that letter. This intervention created, artificially, a summary of this tractate that was so compressed that it first led us into mistakes, until the moment when we noticed that the pages were out of order.

I noticed that all these seemingly arbitrary overhauls could have resulted in a promoter-illusionist still having a substantial number of the lower fragments of the Letter of Peter, as well as of others of "James" and the Gospel of Judas, plus some upper portions where their mutilation had made the pagination disappear, and making from it a small supplementary packet to sell. The packet would be decorated by placing the folio 31/32 on top, which was missing from the text we had. Just such a decorated page (colophon) appeared mysteriously in the catalog of a roving religious exhibition in the United States, showing a page that should be numbered [32], containing the final title "James" (but quite shortened in relation to its "brother" of Nag Hammadi Codex V; here it is merely "James," without the mention of any "Revelation" or "Apocalypse"). The interpretations of these obvious rearrangements remain, of course, in the domain of suspicions, but if they can shock the purchasers of these missing pieces, we might be able to recover those scattered fragments to make the codex complete.

Paris Announcement

With the express authorization of the Maecenas Foundation, on July 1, 2004, in Paris at the Eighth Congress of the International Association for Coptic Studies, I announced the discovery, for the first time, of a copy (in Coptic) of "Judas's famous gospel" (mentioned by St. Irenaeus in his treatise *Against Heresies,* around the year 180, but completely hidden since then). Before the end of 2006, the *editio princeps* of all texts of Codex Tchacos is to be published. The edition will contain top-quality full-size color photographs of all the pages of this codex. These will be supplemented by the reproduction, also in color, of those fragments of papyrus (unfortunately very numerous) that, during the reasonable time granted by Maecenas to avoid delaying too long the publication of the already relatively legible written surfaces, have not yet been placed. These pieces will not be fully identified and placed in their place of origin without considerable future efforts. Thus, identified or not, no remnant of this famous codex will be excluded from its *editio princeps*. These fragments, irreplaceable because of their authenticity, will remain in waiting in this photographic conservatory, because, little by little, they will be identified by zealous and shrewd readers during the future decades. Generations to come will also possess more efficient methods and techniques than ours today.

One of the processes we have used to identify the remnants is the meticulous cutting, requiring infinite patience, of the color photographs of these precious fragments. The cutting has been done by volunteering hands belonging to Mireille Mathys, Serenella Meister, and Bettina Roberty. Having participated in this manner to the resurrection of Codex Tchacos, they also deserve the full recognition of the researchers that, from now on, will enjoy access to the text. While we are thanking all persons of goodwill who have contributed generously to our work but aren't mentioned on the title page, it would be unfair to omit the name of Michel Kasser, who has helped to solve various problems of decipherment of difficult photographic documents and who has prepared the English version of preliminary comments originally edited in French.

After my announcement, I waited for reactions of the audience, but only one, James Robinson asked to speak. One of the most formidable organizers of working teams in gnostic studies, he publicly cautioned me to inquire about the existence of photographs of the codex that had been circulating in the United States for the last twenty years and which might contain part of the text that Maecenas was missing. This public warning had little effect in Paris, and most American and Canadian scholars I met there declared that they were not aware of such a situation.

But some months later, in December 2004, another American Coptologist, Charles Hedrick, greatly committed in research and publications to gnostic scholarship, sent me his transcription and translation of the lower and main fragments of pages 40 and 54–62 of the codex. The same paragraphs were simultaneously published on the Internet. These transcriptions had been made from photographs he had received. He didn't name his source, or the date when he had obtained these photographs, but the published documents bore in the upper right-hand corner of the pages the following handwritten identification: "Transcription – translation – Gospel of Judas – 9 Sept 2001 – ... – photographs Bruce Ferrini." This proves that the American antiquarian had failed in his agreement of February 2001 with Frieda Tchacos Nussberger by not having delivered *all photos* and documentation he had of the codex. Moreover, it also suggests that, contrary to scholarly prudence, Ferrini or someone with access to the codex had forced open the codex in various places to photograph ten "good pages," thus accelerating its fragmentation. How many hours have been wasted to repair (or, more often, to attempt to repair) damage that should never have occurred! Herb

Krosney's book has a more detailed account of the sufferings of the codex.

Still, the text of the Gospel of Judas presented in this edition, although incomplete, offers to anyone interested in this apocryphal work a largely coherent message, whatever the textual losses due to the bad treatment of Codex Tchacos. Judas has endured the dogged ignorance of some of our contemporaries. It has suffered a material loss by erosion estimated at 10 to 15 percent. However, its message has survived largely intact. We have today a clear enough understanding of the "Gospel" or "statement" conveyed a long time ago by this voice lost to world literature, thanks to a conjunction of luck and acts of goodwill and in spite of evident ethical failures. Such a spirit is not always obvious in these materialistic times, through which our soul tries to pave a track of hope. Yet a priceless document that was nearly lost to us has at last been saved.

It gives us reasons to laugh, as does the august Jesus put onstage in this literary creation of a very unusual kind. We smile at the educational dialogues of the "Master" (Rabbi) with his disciples of limited spiritual intelligence, and even with the most gifted among them, the human hero of this "Gospel," Judas the misunderstood—whatever are his weaknesses. We also have reasons to smile rather than to moan at the message previously lost to us, today miraculously resuscitated, emerging from its long silence.

CHRISTIANITY TURNED ON ITS HEAD:
THE ALTERNATIVE VISION
OF THE GOSPEL OF JUDAS

Bart D. Ehrman

I t is not every day that a biblical discovery rocks the world of scholars and laypeople alike, making front-page news throughout Europe and America. The last time it happened was over a generation ago. The Dead Sea Scrolls were discovered in 1947, and yet they continue to be discussed in the news and to play a role in our collective popular imagination still today. They are featured prominently—just to pick an obvious example—in Dan Brown's best-selling novel *The Da Vinci Code*. As it turns out, what Brown has to say about the Dead Sea Scrolls is wrong: The Scrolls do not contain any gospels about Jesus or indeed any reference at all to early Christianity or its founder. They are Jewish books, significant because they revolutionized our understanding of what Judaism was like in its formative years, the years that also marked the beginnings of Christianity.

Even more prominent in Dan Brown's novel are documents discovered just a year and half before the Dead Sea Scrolls, texts that do mention Jesus and that are directly germane to our understanding of early Christianity. These are the gnostic writings discovered near Nag Hammadi, Egypt, in December 1945 by a group of illiterate farmhands digging for fertilizer. Hidden in a jar buried near a boulder next to a cliff face, these writings include previously unknown gospels— books that allegedly record the teachings of Jesus himself, in words quite different from those of the New Testament. Some of these gospels are anonymous, including one called the Gospel of Truth. Others were allegedly written by Jesus' closest followers, including the Gospel of Philip and, most remarkably, the Gospel of Thomas, which consists of 114 sayings of Jesus, many of them previously unknown.

The Gospel of Thomas may well be the most outstanding discovery of Christian antiquity in modern times. But now another gospel has appeared, one that rivals Thomas for its inherent intrigue. This one is also connected with one of Jesus' closest intimates and contains teachings far removed from those that eventually came to be canonized in the writings of the New Testament. In this instance, however, we are not talking about a disciple known for his undying devotion to Jesus. Just the contrary—it is the one disciple reputed to be his mortal enemy and ultimate betrayer, Judas Iscariot.

For centuries, there were rumors that such a gospel existed, but we did not know what it contained until recently. Its reappearance will rank among the greatest finds from Christian antiquity and is without doubt the most important archaeological discovery of the past sixty years.

The various other artifacts unearthed since the Nag Hammadi findings of 1945 have been interesting almost exclusively to scholars wanting to know more about the beginning years of Christianity. The Gospel of Judas, on the other hand, will be fascinating to the non-scholar as well, for this gospel is centered on a figure who is widely known, much maligned, and broadly speculated about. So many questions have circulated about Judas over the years, both among scholars and in the popular imagination: Witness the Broadway hit *Jesus Christ Superstar* and the Hollywood production *The Last Temptation of Christ*.

What will make the newly discovered gospel famous—or infamous, perhaps—is that it portrays Judas quite differently from anything we previously knew. Here he is not the evil, corrupt, devil-inspired follower of Jesus who betrayed his master by handing him over to his enemies. He is instead Jesus' closest intimate and friend, the one who understood Jesus better than anyone else, who turned Jesus over to the authorities because Jesus *wanted* him to do so. In handing him over, Judas performed the greatest service imaginable. According to this gospel, Jesus wanted to escape this material world that stands opposed to God and return to his heavenly home.

This gospel has a completely different understanding of God, the world, Christ, salvation, human existence—not to mention of Judas himself—than came to be embodied in the Christian creeds and canon. It will open up new vistas for understanding Jesus and the religious movement he founded.

OUR EARLIER KNOWLEDGE OF THE GOSPEL

Most people today know of four and only four accounts of the life and death of Jesus—those of Matthew, Mark, Luke, and John, the four gospels of the New Testament. But as has become more widely recognized, even outside the world of scholarship, many other gospels were written during the early centuries of the Christian Church.

Most of these alternate gospels were eventually destroyed as heretical—that is, for teaching the "wrong ideas"—or were lost in antiquity out of general lack of interest. There is no lack of interest in these gospels today, however. Finding them and learning what they have to say has become the obsession of numerous scholars.

We don't know exactly how many gospels were written about Jesus in the first two hundred years or so of Christianity. The four in the New Testament are the oldest ones to survive. But many others were written soon after these four—including the gospels of Thomas and Philip that I mentioned already, the Gospel of Mary—Mary Magdalene—discovered in 1896 but recently drawing a good deal of interest, and now the Gospel of Judas.

We aren't sure when this gospel was written. The copy in our possession appears to date from the end of the third century—around 280 or so (250 years after Jesus' death). But that doesn't tell us when the book was originally composed. In the case of the Gospel of Mark, for example, we don't have any surviving copies until after the third century, but Mark, most likely the first of the canonical gospels to be written, was almost certainly composed by 65 or 70. The earlier copies have all been lost, worn out, or destroyed. So too with the earlier copies of the Gospel of Judas.

We know that this gospel must have been written at least a hundred years before this surviving third- or fourth-century copy was produced, because it was targeted by one of the great authors of the early Christian Church: Irenaeus, the bishop of Lugdunum in Gaul (Lyon in modern France), writing around 180. Irenaeus is one of the earliest and best-known heresiologists (heresy hunters) from Christian antiquity. He wrote a five-volume work that attacked "heretics" (those who held to false doctrines) and advanced a point of view that he considered to be "orthodox" (correct belief). In this work, he named a number of heretical groups, discussed their heretical views, and attacked their heretical writings. One of the false writings he names was a Gospel of Judas.

The heretics that Irenaeus found most dangerous to Christian orthodoxy were the gnostics. To make sense of what Irenaeus has to say about the Gospel of Judas in particular, we must first understand what the gnostic religions believed, and understand why one of these religions hailed Judas as a great hero of the faith rather than the enemy of Christ.

THE GNOSTIC RELIGIONS

Prior to the discovery of the gnostic writings at Nag Hammadi in 1945, Irenaeus was one of our chief sources of information about the various gnostic groups of the second century. Since the Nag Hammadi discovery, scholars have come to dispute whether Irenaeus either knew what he was talking about or presented the views of his opponents fairly. This is because the religious outlook in the Nag Hammadi documents differs in some key ways from Irenaeus's defamatory descriptions. But by reading his book judiciously, and giving full credit to the firsthand accounts of the newly discovered writings themselves—which were, after all, written by gnostics for gnostics—we can piece together a good deal of what the various gnostic religions espoused.

I should say at the outset that there were a large number of gnostic religions, and they differed from one another in lots of ways, large and small. So great was their variety that some scholars have insisted that we shouldn't even use the term gnosticism any more—that it's an umbrella term not large enough to cover all the religious diversity found among its alleged groups.

My own view is that this is going too far, that it is perfectly legitimate to talk about gnosticism, just as it is legitimate to talk about Judaism or about Christianity even though there are enormous differences among the kinds of Judaism or Christianity found in the world today, let alone in antiquity. For the specific kind of gnosticism that the Gospel of Judas represents, I can refer you to the excellent essay by Marvin Meyer in this collection, where he explains the gospel in terms of the sect known as the Sethian gnostics. But here let me explain in broad terms what the various and wide-ranging gnostic sects held in common and why ortho-dox writers such as Irenaeus found them so threatening.

The term *gnosticism* comes from the Greek word *gnōsis,* which means knowledge. Gnostics are those who are "in the know." And what is it that they know? They know secrets that can bring salvation. For gnostics, a person is saved not by having faith in Christ or by doing good works. Rather, a person is saved by knowing the truth—the truth about the world we live in, about who the true God is, and especially about who we ourselves are. In other words, this is largely self-knowledge: Knowledge of where we came from, how we got here, and how we can return to our heavenly home. According to most gnostics, this material world is *not* our home. We are trapped here, in these bodies of flesh, and we need to learn how to escape. For those gnostics who were also Christian (many gnostics were not), it is Christ himself who brings this secret knowledge from above. He reveals the truth to his intimate followers, and it is this truth that can set them free.

Traditional Christianity has taught, of course, that our world is the good creation of the one true God. But this was not the view of the gnostics. According to a wide range of gnostic groups, the god who created this world is not the only god and in fact is not even the most powerful or all-knowing god. He is a much lesser, inferior, and often ignorant deity. How can anyone look at this world and call it good? Gnostics saw the disasters around them—the earthquakes, hurricanes, floods, famines, droughts, epidemics, misery, suffering—and they declared that the world is not good. But, they said, you can't pin the blame of this world on God! No, this world is a cosmic disaster, and salvation comes only to those who learn how to escape this world and its material trappings.

Some gnostic thinkers explained this evil, material world by expounding complicated myths of creation. According to these myths, the ultimate divine being is completely removed from the world, in that he is absolutely spirit—with no material aspects or qualities. This divine being generated lots of offspring known as *aeons* who, like him, were spiritual entities. Originally this divine realm, inhabited by God and his aeons, was all that existed. But a cosmic catastrophe occurred in which one of these aeons somehow fell from the divine realm, leading to the creation of other divine beings who therefore came into existence outside of the divine sphere. These lesser divine beings created our material world. They made the world as a place of entrapment for sparks of divinity that they had captured, to be placed within human bodies. Some humans, in other words, have an element of the divine within them, at their core. These people don't have mortal souls, but immortal souls, temporarily imprisoned in this capricious and miserable realm of matter. And those souls need to escape, to return to the divine realm whence they came.

The myths narrated by the various gnostic groups differed widely from one another in many of their details. And they are nothing if not detailed. For modern readers, these myths can be highly confusing and bizarre. But their overriding point is clear: This world is not the creation of the one true God. The god who made this world—the God of the Old Testament—is a secondary, inferior deity. He is not the God above all who is to be worshiped. Rather, he is to be avoided, by learning the truth about the ultimate divine realm, this evil material world, our entrapment here, and how we can escape.

I should stress that not everyone has the means to escape. That is because not everyone has a spark of the divine within them: Only some of us do. The other people are the creations of the inferior god of this world. They, like other creatures here (dogs, turtles, mosquitoes, and so on), will die and that will be the end of their story. But some of us are trapped divinities. And we need to learn how to return to our heavenly home.

How can we learn the secret knowledge necessary for our salvation? We obviously can't learn it by looking around at the world and figuring it out for ourselves. Learning about this world imparts nothing more than knowledge of the material creation of an inferior deity who is not the true God. Instead, we need to have a revelation bestowed upon us from on high. There needs to be an emissary from the spiritual realm who comes to us to tell us the truth about our origin, our destination, and our means of escape. In Christian gnostic religions, the one who comes from above to reveal this truth is Christ. According to this understanding, Christ was not merely a mortal with wise religious teachings. Nor is he the son of the creator god, the God of the Old Testament.

Some gnostics taught that Christ was an aeon from the realm above—that he was not a man of flesh and blood, born into this world of the creator, but that he came from above only in the *appearance* of human flesh. He was a phantasm who took on the appearance of flesh to teach those who were called (i.e., the gnostics, who have the spark within) the secret truths they need for salvation.

Other gnostics taught that Jesus was a real man, but that he did not have a typical spark of the divine within. His soul was a special divine being who came from above to be temporarily housed within the man Jesus, to use him as a conduit through which to reveal the necessary truths to his close followers. In this understanding, the divine element came into Jesus at some point of his life—for example, at his baptism, when the Spirit descended upon him—and then left him once his ministry was over. That would explain why, on the cross, Jesus cried out, "My God, my God, why have you abandoned me?" It was because the divine element within him had left prior to his crucifixion, since, after all, the divine cannot suffer and die.

Heresy hunters like Irenaeus found gnostics particularly insidious and difficult to attack. The problem was that you couldn't reason with a gnostic to show him the error of his ways: He had secret knowledge that you didn't! If you said that he was wrong, he could shrug it off and point out that you simply didn't know. And so Irenaeus and others like him had to pull out all the stops in their attacks, trying to convince other Christians, at least, that the gnostics did not have the truth, but had actually perverted the truth by rejecting the God of the Old Testament and his creation and by denying that Christ really was a flesh-and-blood human being, whose death and resurrection (not his secret teachings) brought salvation. Irenaeus's five-volume refutation of gnostics maligned their beliefs for being hopelessly contradictory, ridiculously detailed, and contrary to the teachings of Jesus' own apostles. He sometimes referred to some of the gnostic writings in order to poke fun at them, contrasting them to the sacred Scriptures accepted by the Church at large. One of the writings he mocked was the Gospel of Judas.

Gnostic Cainites and the Gospel of Judas

One of the many gnostic groups that Irenaeus discussed was called the Cainites. We don't know if this group really existed or if Irenaeus simply made their name up—there is no independent record of their existence. However, one of the things Irenaeus says about the Cainites is that they supported their aberrant beliefs by appealing to the Gospel of Judas.

The group was named after Cain, the first son of Adam and Eve. Cain is notorious in the annals of biblical history for being the first fratricide. He was jealous of his younger brother Abel, who was especially beloved of God, and so Cain murdered him (Genesis 4). Why would the Cainites choose him, of all people, as a hero of their faith? It is because they believed that the God of the Old Testament was not the true God to be worshiped, but was the ignorant creator of this world who needed to be escaped. And so, all the figures in Jewish and Christian history who stood against God—Cain, the men of Sodom and Gomorrah, and eventually Judas Iscariot—were the ones who had seen the truth and understood the secrets necessary for salvation.

According to Irenaeus, the Cainites took their opposition to the Old Testament god to an ethical extreme. Anything that God commanded, they opposed, and anything that God opposed, they supported. If God says to keep the Sabbath, not to eat pork, and not to commit adultery—then the way to show your freedom from God was to ignore the Sabbath, eat pork, and commit adultery!

It is not surprising to learn that a gnostic group with such an inverted view would naturally regard Jesus' alleged enemy as his greatest ally. According to Irenaeus, the Cainites had the Gospel of Judas as their authority. According to this gospel, Irenaeus tells us, Judas alone among the disciples understood the message of Jesus and did as Jesus himself wanted—turning him over to the authorities for his crucifixion. Judas was thus seen as the ultimate follower of Jesus, one whose actions should be emulated rather than spurned. For he was the one to whom Jesus had delivered the secret knowledge necessary for salvation.

The Gospel of Judas published here is almost certainly this gospel cited by Irenaeus in 180. Scholars will differ on when it was first composed, but most will probably date it to 140-160 or so. It was written at a time when gnostic religions were starting to thrive in the Christian Church, and it had been around some years before Irenaeus began his assault on them. That this is the gospel Irenaeus knew is confirmed by its contents. For in this gospel Judas is the only disciple who understands who Jesus really is, and he is the only disciple to whom Jesus delivers his secret revelation that can lead to salvation. The other disciples worship the God of the Old Testament, and so are "ministers of error." Because Judas knows the truth, he performs the greatest service for Jesus: handing him over to be executed so that the divine being within Jesus can escape the trappings of his material body. Or as Jesus puts it so cogently in this gospel: "You [Judas] will exceed all of them [i.e., the other disciples]. For you will sacrifice the man that clothes me."

What is the distinctive portrayal of Judas in this gospel? How does its overall religious perspective differ from the "orthodox" views that came to be embraced by the majority of Christians? And why was it, and other books like it, eventually excluded from the canon of Christian scripture?

Portrayal of Judas in the Gospel

There are several people named Judas in the New Testament—just as there are several Marys, several Herods, and several named James. Since so many of them had the same name—and since lower-class people never had last names—these various persons had to be distinguished from one another in some way. Usually this was done by indicating where they came from or to whom they were related. For example, the different Marys are called Mary the mother of Jesus, Mary of Bethany, Mary Magdalene, and so forth. Among those named Judas—or Jude, as the name is sometimes translated—one was an actual brother of Jesus (Matthew 13:55); another was a disciple, Judas the son of James (Luke 6:16); and yet a third was a different disciple, Judas Iscariot. Scholars have long debated what "Iscariot" is supposed to mean, and no one knows for sure. It may refer to Judas's hometown, a village in Judea (the southern part of modern Israel) called Kerioth ("Ish-Kerioth," or Iscariot, would mean "man from Kerioth"). In any event, when I refer to Judas here in this discussion, it will always be to this one, Judas Iscariot.

Judas in the Gospels of the New Testament
Judas's betrayal is not portrayed as an ignominious act

in the Gospel of Judas. But in the New Testament gospels, this is his distinguishing mark. Among the twelve disciples, he is the bad apple. Judas is mentioned some twenty times in these books, and in every instance the gospel writers have something hostile to say about him, usually simply pointing out that he was Jesus' betrayer. They all assume this was a very evil deed.

Readers over the years have wondered about that. If Jesus had to die on the cross for the salvation of the world, then wasn't Judas doing a *good* deed in handing him over? Without the betrayal there would be no arrest, without the arrest there would be no trial, without the trial there would be no crucifixion, without the crucifixion there would be no resurrection—and in short, we *still* wouldn't be saved from our sins. So why were Judas's actions such a bad thing?

Our gospel writers never address that speculative question. They simply assume that Judas betrayed the cause and his master, and that even though good came out of it, his act was a damnable offense: "It would have been better for that man never to have been born!" (Mark 14:21).

These accounts provide different explanations for why Judas betrayed Jesus. In the first of our Gospels, Mark, we're given no explanation of the deed at all: Judas goes to the Jewish leaders volunteering to betray

Jesus, and they agree to give him some money in exchange (Mark 14:10–11). It may be that Judas wanted the money, but Mark doesn't say that was his motivation. The Gospel of Matthew, written some years after Mark, is more explicit: In this version, Judas approaches the Jewish leaders to see how much he can make off of his act of betrayal; they settle the amount at thirty pieces of silver, and he keeps his end of the bargain. Here Judas simply wants the cash (Matthew 26:14–16). The Gospel of Luke was written at about the same time as Matthew, and now an additional factor is thrown in. According to Luke, Satan—the ultimate enemy of God—entered into Judas and drove him to do the dirty deed (Luke 22:3). In this account, Judas could say, "The Devil made me do it." Our final gospel is John, and here we learn that Jesus knew all along that "one of you [i.e., one of the disciples] is a devil" (John 6:70). Moreover, we're told that Judas had been entrusted with the group's purse (John 12:4–6) and commonly used to dip into it for his own purposes. For this gospel, then, Judas is driven both by his own demonic nature and by greed.

What is it, exactly, that Judas betrayed to the authorities? On this the New Testament gospels appear to agree. Jesus and his disciples had come from the northern part of the land to the capital city, Jerusalem, in order to celebrate the annual Passover feast. This was a big deal in Jerusalem at the time, as during the festival the city would swell many times over as pilgrims from around the world came together to worship God in commemoration of the act of salvation he had performed, many centuries before, when he spared the children of the Israelites from death and delivered them out of Egypt. Because of the enormous crowds, there was always the fear of religious enthusiasm growing to a fevered pitch and riots breaking out. The authorities were particularly afraid that Jesus was a troublemaker, and they wanted to have him arrested when he was isolated from the crowds, quietly, so that they could dispose of him without creating a major disturbance. Judas was the one who told them how they could do it. He led them to Jesus in the dead of night when he was alone, with his disciples, praying. The authorities made the secret arrest, put Jesus on trial before a kangaroo court, and had him crucified before any real resistance could be organized.

What happened afterward to Judas is recounted by only two of our gospel writers. Most famously, according to the Gospel of Matthew, Judas was filled with remorse, returned the thirty pieces of silver to the Jewish high priests, and went out to hang himself. They realized they could not use the returned money for the Temple coffers, since it had been used to betray innocent blood. And so they purchased a field with it to use for the burial of strangers. The field was called a potter's field—possibly because it contained red clay popular among the potters in town. It came then to be known as the "Field of Blood" because it had been purchased with "blood money."

Mark and John don't say anything about Judas's demise; nor does the Gospel of Luke. But in the book of Acts—written by the author of Luke, as a kind of sequel to his gospel—we learn another version of Judas's death, also tied to a field in Jerusalem. In this case, however, Judas himself is said to have owned the field and to have died on it. Here he does not hang himself. Instead, he bursts forth in the midst (i.e., his stomach rips open) and he spills his intestines on the ground, creating a bloody mess. It is for *that* reason it is called the "Field of Blood" (Acts 1:15–19). This does not appear to be a suicide, as in Matthew, but an act of God, who brings Judas to a gory end in just retribution for his evil deed.

All of these accounts stand in stark contrast with what we find in the Gospel of Judas. Here Judas's deed is not evil. Instead, what he does is the will of God, as explained to him in secret revelations by Jesus himself. By making it possible for Jesus to die, Judas allows the divine spark within Jesus to escape the material trappings of his body to return to his heavenly home. Judas is the hero, not the villain.

Judas in the Gospel of Judas

In the opening words of this newly recovered gospel, it becomes clear that the portrayal of Judas will not be at all like that found in the New Testament, and that the account that follows will contain a gnostic perspective on his deed. The text begins by saying that it is "the secret account of the revelation that Jesus spoke in conversation with Judas Iscariot." Off the bat, then, we're told that this is a "secret" account—it is not for everyone, but only for those who are in the know, that is, for "gnostics." The account conveys a revelation given by Jesus, the divine emissary who alone can reveal the truth necessary for salvation. And to whom does he reveal it? Not to the crowds who flock to hear him teach, not even to the twelve disciples he has called around him. He reveals the secret to Judas Iscariot alone, his most intimate companion, and the only one in this gospel who understands the real truth of Jesus.

The next time Judas is mentioned in the text is when Jesus challenges the twelve disciples to show whether or not they are "perfect" (that is, capable of salvation) and stand before him. The disciples all claim that they have the strength to do so, but in fact only Judas is able to stand—and even he has to turn his face away. This must mean that Judas has the spark of the divine within him, so that he is in some sense on a par with Jesus, but he has not yet come to understand the secret truth that Jesus is about to reveal, and so he averts his eyes. But Judas does know Jesus' true identity—something the others are completely blind to—for Judas proclaims that Jesus is not a mere mortal from this world. He comes from the divine world above: "You are from the immortal realm of Barbelo," he says. As Marvin Meyer explains, according to Sethian gnostics, Barbelo is one of the primary divine beings in the perfect realm of the true God. That is where Jesus has come from—not from this world created by a secondary, inferior deity.

Because Judas has correctly perceived Jesus' character, Jesus takes him aside, away from the ignorant others, to teach him "the mysteries of the kingdom." Judas alone will receive the secret knowledge necessary for salvation. And Jesus informs him that he will attain this salvation—even though he will grieve in the process. He will grieve because he will be rejected by "the twelve," who will elect someone to take his place. This is a reference to what happens in the New Testament book of Acts, when after Judas's death, the eleven disciples replace him with Matthias so they can remain twelve in number (Acts 1:16–26). For the Gospel of Judas, this is a good thing—not for the twelve, but for Judas. He is the one who can attain salvation, while the other apostles continue to be concerned about "their god," that is, the creator god of the Old Testament, whom both Jesus and Judas can transcend.

This theme is replayed later in the text, when Judas recounts to Jesus a "great vision" that he has seen that has troubled him. In this vision he saw the twelve disciples (evidently the eleven others and the one who eventually would replace him) stoning him to death. But then he saw a great house filled with magnificent people. Judas wants to enter that house—for the house represents the divine realm where the immortal spirits dwell in eternal harmony. Jesus informs him that no one who is born of mortals can enter that house: It "is reserved for the holy." But as we will later learn in the text, this means that everyone who—like Judas—has a spark of the divine within will be allowed entrance once they have escaped their mortal flesh.

Judas's impending death, in other words, will not be a great tragedy, even though he might find it grievous at the time. Upon his death he will become the "thirteenth," that is, he will be outside the twelve disciples and will transcend their number. He alone will be able to enter into the divine realm symbolized by the great house of his vision. And so he will "be cursed by the other generation," by the race of mortals who are not destined for ultimate salvation. At the same time, he "will come to rule over them," for he will be far superior to all in this material world once he has attained to his salvation, based on the secret knowledge that Jesus is about to reveal.

A good portion of the surviving gospel contains the secret revelation that Jesus delivers to Judas alone. It reveals "a great and boundless eternal realm"—the realm of the truly divine beings beyond this world and far above the inferior deities who created this material existence and humans. The revelation will strike many modern readers as inordinately complex and difficult to understand. But its basic thrust is clear. Numerous superior divine beings came into existence long before the gods of this world appeared. The gods of this world include El (the word for "God" in the Old Testament); his helper Nebro, also called Yaldabaoth, who is defiled with blood and whose name means "rebel"; and another named Saklas, a word that means "fool." Thus the deities in charge of this world are the Old Testament God, a bloody rebel, and a fool. This is not a ringing endorsement of the world's creator(s).

Saklas, the fool, is said to be the one who creates humans "after the [his own?] image," which leads Judas to question: Is it possible for humans to transcend life in this world? As we will see later, the answer is a qualified yes. Some humans have an element of the divine within. They will survive to transcend this world, to enter into the divine realm far above the bloodthirsty, foolish creator gods.

Judas himself is the first to do so. We're told near the end of the text that he has his wish fulfilled: He enters into "the luminous cloud" which represents, in this text, the world of the true God and his aeons. Like everyone else, Judas has a guiding "star" (see Marvin Meyer's essay). His star is superior to all the others. His star "leads the way."

It leads to his proper understanding of all that Jesus has taught him. Salvation does not come by worshiping the God of this world or accepting his creation. It comes by denying this world and rejecting the body that binds us to it. That is the ultimate reason why the deed that Judas performs for Jesus is a righteous act, one that earns him the right to surpass all the others. By handing Jesus over to the authorities, Judas allows Jesus to escape his own mortal flesh to return to his eternal home. We have already seen Jesus say, "You will exceed all of them. For you will sacrifice the man that clothes me."

The betrayal scene itself is told in muted terms, and it differs in a number of ways from the accounts found in the New Testament. Here Jesus is not outside, praying in the Garden of Gethsemane, for example. He is indoors, in a "guest room." As in the New Testament gospels, the Jewish leaders, here called "the scribes," want to arrest Jesus privately, "for they were afraid of the people, since he was regarded by all as a prophet." But when they see Judas, they are surprised: "What are you doing here? You are Jesus' disciple." These leaders too do not understand the truth, that to truly serve Jesus means to hand him over to the authorities so that he can be executed. Judas gives them the response they want to hear, they give him some money for the deed, and he hands Jesus over. And that's where the gospel ends, with what for this author was the climax of the account: not Jesus' death and resurrection, but the faithful act of his most intimate companion and faithful follower, the one who handed him over to his death that he might return to his heavenly home.

Unusual Theological Views of the Gospel of Judas

We have already noted some of the key theological themes of this gospel: The creator of this world is not the one true God; this world is an evil place to be escaped; Christ is not the son of the creator; salvation comes not through the death and resurrection of Jesus, but through the revelation of secret knowledge that he provides. These themes stand diametrically opposed to the theological views that eventually triumphed in the early Christian debates concerning proper belief—that is to say, in the theological wars of the second and third centuries, when different Christian groups maintained different systems of belief and doctrine, all of them insisting that their views were not only right but were the views of Jesus and his closest followers.

We have long known about these debates, and the Gospel of Judas allows us to see one side of them even more clearly—one of the sides that ended up losing. Every side laid claim to sacred books supporting its point of view; all insisted that these views came straight from Jesus, and through him from God. But only one side won. This was the side that decided which books should be considered Scripture, and that wrote the Christian creeds that have come down to us today. Embodied in these creeds are theological statements that trumpet the success of the "orthodox" party. Consider the opening of one of the most famous of these creeds:

We believe in one God, the Father, the almighty,
maker of heaven and earth,
of all things visible and invisible.

This affirmation stands in stark contrast with the views set forth in the Gospel of Judas, where there is not just one God but many gods and where the creator of this world is not the true God but an inferior deity, who is not the Father of all and is certainly not almighty.

We are now in a position to examine more closely some of the key teachings of this gospel, its views about God, the world, Christ, salvation, and the other apostles who stand behind the creed that came to be accepted as authoritative yet who never do understand the truth.

The View of God in the Gospel

At the outset of the gospel it is clear that the God of Jesus is not the creator god of the Jews. In one of the opening scenes, Jesus finds the disciples gathered together "in pious observance." Literally the Coptic says that the disciples were "engaged in practices with respect to God." They were sharing a eucharistic meal, in which they were thanking God for their food. One would expect Jesus to respect this religious act. But instead he begins to laugh. The disciples don't see what is funny: "Why are you laughing at our prayer of thanksgiving? We have done what is right." Jesus replies that they don't know what they are really doing: By giving thanks for their food, they are praising *their* god—that is, not the God of Jesus. Now the disciples are befuddled: "Master, you are ... the son of our god." No, as it turns out, he is not. Jesus responds that no one of their "generation" will know who he really is.

The disciples do not take kindly to this rebuke and "start getting angry and raging and blaspheming against him in their hearts." Jesus proceeds to upbraid them and speaks again about "your god who is within you." At play here are several key themes, which repeat throughout the narrative: The disciples of Jesus do not know who he really is; they worship a God who is not Jesus' father; they don't understand the truth about God. Judas, the only one who truly understands, declares that Jesus has come from "the immortal realm of Barbelo," that is, from the realm of the true immortal divine beings, not from the lower realm of the creator god of the Jews.

This understanding of the creator god as an inferior deity is most clearly stated in the myth that Jesus expounds privately to Judas later in the text. According to proto-orthodox writers such as Irenaeus (I call him "proto-orthodox" because he embraced views that at a later date would come to be called orthodox), there is only one God and he is the one who made all that exists, in heaven and earth. Not for this text, though. The complexities of the myth that Jesus reveals to Judas may seem befuddling, but its gist is clear. Even before the creator god came into being, there were enormous numbers of other divine beings: seventy-two aeons, each with a "luminary" and each with five firmaments of the heavens (for a total of 360 firmaments), along with countless angels worshiping each one. Moreover, this world belongs to the realm of "perdition" or, as the word could also be translated, "corruption." It is not the good creation of the one true God. Only after all the other divine entities come into existence does the God of the Old Testament—named El—come into being, followed by his helpers, the blood-stained rebel Yaldabaoth and the fool Saklas. These latter two created the world, and then humans.

When the disciples worship "their God," it is the rebel and fool they worship, the makers of this bloody, senseless material existence. They do not worship the true God, the one who is above all else, who is all-knowing, all-powerful, entirely spirit, and completely removed from this transient world of pain and suffering created by a rebel and a fool. It is no wonder that Irenaeus found this text so offensive. It claimed to represent the views of Jesus, yet its views are a complete mockery of Irenaeus's most cherished beliefs.

The View of Christ

Throughout this text, Jesus speaks of the twelve disciples and "their God." It is clear that Jesus does not belong to the god of this world—one of his goals, in fact, is to reveal the inferiority and moral turpitude of this god, before returning to the divine realm, the perfect world of the Spirit, after leaving his mortal body.

For this text, then, Jesus is not a normal human being. The first indication of this is that he "appeared" on earth. This already suggests that he came from another realm. And since he spends much of the gospel revealing the "secret mysteries" about the immortal world of true divinity, the natural assumption is that this other realm is where he originated.

His unique character is hinted at in the next comment about him: "Often he did not appear to his disciples as himself, but he was found among them as a child." Scholars who are familiar with a range of early Christian literature will have no trouble understanding this allusion. A number of Christian writings outside the New Testament portray Jesus as a "docetic" being—that is, as one who looked human only because it was an appearance (*docetic* comes from the Greek word *dokeō*, which means to "seem" or to "appear"). As a divine being, Jesus could take on whatever shape he wanted. In some early Christian writings, Jesus could appear as an old man or a child—simultaneously, to different people! (This can be found, for example, in a noncanonical book called the Acts of John.) So too here: Jesus did not have a real fleshly body, but could assume different appearances at will.

But why would he appear to the disciples as a child? Wouldn't this appearance undercut rather than assert his authority over them? (He's just a child, what does *he* know?) This point will no doubt be debated by scholars of the text for a long time. It does appear that being a child here is not meant at all in a negative way, but positively: Children are unspoiled by the harsh realities of this material world and uncorrupted by its false wisdom. Moreover, doesn't the Bible itself indicate, "Out of the mouth of babes and infants you have established strength" (Psalm 8:2)? The child represents purity and innocence before the world. And Christ alone embodied absolute purity—and wisdom and knowledge that transcend the mere mortal.

This knowledge is, of course, the main theme of the Gospel of Judas. It is the knowledge of the secret mysteries that Jesus alone has and that Judas alone is worthy to hear. Jesus has this knowledge because he comes from the "realm of Barbelo." And he is apparently able to visit that realm at will. The day after his first conversation with the disciples, they want to know where he had gone in the meantime, and he tells them, "I went to another great and holy generation." When they ask him about that "generation," he laughs again—this time not at their ignorant worship of the creator but at their lack of knowledge about the realm of the truly divine. For no mere mortal can go there—it is a realm beyond this world, the realm of all perfection and truth, the ultimate destination of those who contain an element of the divine that can escape the trappings of this material world. Jesus alone knows about this realm, for that is whence he came and where he will return.

As we have seen, Judas is the most intimate follower of Jesus in this text not only because he is the only one worthy to receive the secret mysteries of that realm, but also because he makes it possible for Jesus to return there permanently. He does this by turning him over to the authorities for execution. Jesus only appears to have a real flesh-and-blood body for his time here on earth in human form. He needs to escape this mortal coil to return to his heavenly home.

What then is the significance of Jesus' death in this gospel? Irenaeus and other proto-orthodox writers based their views on writings that eventually became the New Testament, such as the Gospel of Mark and the letters of the apostle Paul, where Jesus' death is said to be an atoning sacrifice for sins (see Mark 10:45; Romans 3:21–28). In this view, Jesus' death was all-important for salvation: It paid the price of sin so that others—those who committed sins against God—could be restored to a right relationship with the God who created this world and all that is in it. Not so for the Gospel of Judas. In this gospel, there is no need to be reconciled with the creator of this world, who is merely a bloodthirsty rebel. On the contrary, the need is to escape this world and its creator. That happens once one relinquishes the body that belongs to the creator. Jesus' death is his own escape. And when we die, we too can escape.

It will strike many readers as odd that the Gospel of Judas ends where it does, with the so-called betrayal. But it makes perfect sense given the views otherwise advanced in the book. The death of Jesus is a foregone conclusion: All that is needed is the means by which it will occur, and Judas does his part in making sure it will happen. That's why he "exceeds" all the others.

There will be no resurrection. This is perhaps the key point of all. Jesus will not be raised from the dead in this book. Why would he be? The entire point of salvation is to *escape* this material world. A resurrection of a dead corpse brings the person back *into* the world of the creator. Since the point is to allow the soul to leave this world behind and to enter into "that great and holy generation"—that is, the divine realm that transcends this world—a resurrection of the body is the very last thing that Jesus, or any of his true followers, would want.

Views of Salvation
That, of course, is the goal of Jesus' true followers as

well. This world and all its trappings are to be transcended. That can occur when the soul learns the truth of its origin and destination, and then escapes from the material prison of the body.

This teaching becomes clear in a key conversation between Judas and Jesus, in which "this" generation—that is, the race of people here on earth—is contrasted with "that" generation, the realm of the divine beings. Some people belong to this generation, some to that one. Those with the divine element within belong to that one; only they can be saved when they die. When the others—of "this" generation—die, that will be the end of their story. As Jesus says,

> The souls of every human generation will die. When *these* people [i.e., those who belong to the realm above], however, have completed the time of the kingdom and the spirit leaves them, their bodies will die but their souls will be alive, and they will be taken up.

In this way of understanding, humans consist of a body, a spirit, and a soul. The body is the material part that clothes the inner soul, which is the real essence of the person. The spirit is the force that animates the body, giving it life. When the spirit leaves the body, the body dies and ceases to exist. For those who belong only to this human realm, the soul then dies as well. As Jesus later says, "It is impossible to sow seed on [rock] and harvest its fruit." In other words, without a spark of the divine within, there will be no ongoing life. But for those who belong to the realm above, the soul lives on after death and is taken up to its heavenly home.

This idea is further explained after Jesus describes the myth of beginnings to Judas, who wants to know, "Does the human spirit die?" Jesus explains that there are two kinds of human, those whose bodies have been given a spirit on a temporary basis by the archangel Michael, "so that they might offer service," and those who have eternal spirits granted them by the archangel Gabriel, who belong therefore to "the great generation with no ruler over it." These latter are those who have a spark of the divine within them and who, after their death, will return to the realm whence they came. Judas himself, of course, is among them. The other disciples, on the other hand, appear to be of the first kind, who out of ignorance "offer service," but who, upon their deaths, simply cease to exist.

Views of Jesus' Followers
One of the most striking features of the Gospel of Judas is this persistent refrain that the twelve disciples of Jesus never understand the truth, stand outside the

realm of the saved, and persecute Judas—not realizing that he alone both knows and understands Jesus and the secrets he has revealed. It is because they don't know any better, as we have seen, that they stone Judas in a vision. Judas is outside their number, and so Jesus calls him "the thirteenth." Here, thirteen is the lucky number.

The twelve disciples are portrayed as those who worship the creator god, for example, in the eucharist scene that opens the account. This portrayal is even more graphic in a later scene that is regrettably fragmentary, in which the disciples describe to Jesus a vision they have had of the sacrifices taking place in the Temple in Jerusalem.

Many readers will be familiar with the New Testament story of the disciples and Jesus arriving at the Temple just a week before Jesus' execution. Jesus creates a disturbance in the Temple, overthrowing the tables of the money changers and driving out those selling sacrificial animals (Mark 11:15–17). The disciples, on the other hand, are shown as being unduly impressed with what they have seen, as rural Galileans making a trip to the big city for the first time, and overawed by the grandeur and magnitude of the Temple. They exclaim in Mark 13:1, "Master, what large stones and what large buildings!"

The Gospel of Judas presents an alternate version of this scene. Here the disciples comment to Jesus not about the Temple building but about the sacrifices taking place within it. They see an altar, priests, a crowd, and sacrifices being made, and they are disturbed, wanting to know what it is all about. As it turns out, it is all about them. Jesus tells them that the priests at the altar, performing the sacrifices, "invoke my name." In other words, those responsible for this worship of the Jewish God believe that they are serving Jesus himself. We then learn that what the disciples have seen is a symbolic vision—not about the actual Jewish sacrifices in the Temple, but about their own practices of worship. Jesus tells them:

> Those you have seen performing religious duties at the altar—that is who you are. That is the god you serve, and you are those twelve men you have seen. The cattle you have seen brought for sacrifice are the many people you lead astray....

In other words, the disciples who continue to practice their religion as if the ultimate object of worship is the creator god of the Jews, invoking Jesus' name in support of their worship, have gotten it all wrong. Rather than serving the true God they are blaspheming him. And in doing so, they lead their followers astray.

This is a damning portrayal not only of Jesus' disciples, but also of the proto-orthodox Christians living at the time the Gospel of Judas was produced. The proto-orthodox did not, of course, continue to worship in the Jewish Temple. It had been destroyed by this time and the vast majority of the proto-orthodox were Gentiles, not Jews. But they insisted that the God they worshiped was the Jewish God who gave the Jewish law and sent the Jewish Messiah to the Jewish people in fulfillment of the Jewish Scriptures. They understood themselves to be the "true Jews," the true people of the one true God.

Jesus in this gospel indicates that they are completely misled. They do indeed worship the Jewish God. But this god is a reckless fool. He did create this world, but the world is not good; it is a cesspool of misery and suffering. The true God has never had anything to do with this world. This world must be escaped, not embraced. The proto-orthodox Christians are promoting a false religion. Only the religion taught secretly by Jesus to his most intimate follower Judas is ultimately true. All the rest is a sham at best, a noxious error promoted by the leaders of the proto-orthodox churches.

The Gospel of Judas and the Canon of Scripture

In light of its harsh attacks on the proto-orthodox Church leaders—forebears of Irenaeus and other like-minded theologians who developed the "orthodox" way of understanding God, the world, Christ, and salvation—it is no wonder that this Gospel of Judas never had much of a chance of being included in the New Testament. How did we get our our New Testament, with its four gospels of Matthew, Mark, Luke, and John, and why some few Christian writings made it into the canon, but most others (like the Gospel of Judas) were excluded?

The New Testament consists of twenty-seven books that the victorious orthodox party accepted as sacred texts conveying God's word to his people. When Christianity started out—with the historical Jesus himself—it already had a set of sacred written authorities. Jesus was a Jew living in Palestine, and like all Palestinian Jews, he accepted the authority of the Jewish Scriptures, especially the first five books of what Christians have called the Old Testament (Genesis, Exodus, Leviticus, Numbers, and Deuteronomy), sometimes known as the Law of Moses. Jesus presented himself as an authoritative interpreter of these Scriptures and was known to his followers as a great rabbi (teacher).

After Jesus' death, his followers continued to revere his teachings and began to ascribe to them an authority equal to that of Moses himself. Not only Jesus' teachings but also the teachings of his closest followers were seen as authoritative, especially as these came to be written down in books. But as years and decades passed, more and more writings appeared, claiming to have been written by apostles. We have more letters by Paul, for example, than the thirteen that go under his name in the New Testament, and scholars today are reasonably sure that some of those in the New Testament were not actually written by Paul. Similarly, the Apocalypse or Revelation of John appears in the New Testament, but other apocalpyses were left out—for example, an Apocalypse of Peter and an Apocalypse of Paul.

There were lots of gospels. The four in the New Testament are anonymous writings—only in the second century did they come to be called by the names of Jesus' disciples (Matthew and John) and of two companions of the apostles (Mark the companion of Peter; and Luke the companion of Paul). Other gospels appeared that also claimed to be written by apostles. In addition to our newly discovered Gospel of Judas, we have gospels allegedly written by Philip and by Peter, two different gospels by Jesus' brother Judas Thomas, one by Mary Magdalene, and so on.

All of these gospels (and epistles, apocalypses, etc.) were connected with apostles, they all claimed to represent the true teachings of Jesus, and they all were revered—by one Christian group or another—as sacred scripture. As time went on, more and more started to appear. Given the enormous debates that were being waged over the proper interpretation of the religion, how were people to know which books to accept?

In brief, one of the competing groups in Christianity succeeded in overwhelming all the others. This group gained more converts than its opponents and managed to relegate all its competitors to the margins. This group decided what the Church's organizational structure would be. It decided which creeds Christians would recite. And it decided which books would be accepted as Scripture. This was the group to which Irenaeus belonged, as did other figures well known to scholars of second- and third-century Christianity, such as Justin Martyr and Tertullian. This group became "orthodox," and once it had sealed its victory over all of its opponents, it rewrote the history of the engagement—claiming that it had always been the majority opinion of Christianity, that its views had always been the views of the apostolic churches and of the apostles, that its creeds were rooted directly in the teachings of Jesus. The books that it accepted as Scripture proved the point, for Matthew, Mark, Luke, and John all tell the story as the proto-orthodox had grown accustomed to hearing it.

What happened to all the other books, the ones that told a different version of the story and so had been left out of the proto-orthodox canon? Some of them were destroyed, but most were simply lost or crumbled with age. They were rarely, if ever, copied after a while, since their views had been deemed heretical. Only in small marginal groups within Christianity—a gnostic group here, a Jewish Christian group there—were these writings kept alive. Rumors of their existence continued to circulate, but no one was particularly keen to preserve them for posterity. What would be the point? They contained falsehood and would simply lead people astray. Better to let them die an ignoble death.

And so they did. Seldom were they recopied when the old texts wore out, and eventually even these isolated copies disappeared—until modern times, when on rare occasions one of them turns up, to show us anew that the orthodox understanding of religion was not the only one in the second century of Christianity. There was in fact a thriving opposition to this understanding, an opposition embodied, for example, in the recent gem of a discovery, the Gospel of Judas. Here is a book that turns the theology of traditional Christianity on its head and reverses everything we ever thought about the nature of true Christianity. In this book the truth is not taught by the other disciples of Jesus and their proto-orthodox successors. These Christian leaders are blind to the truth, which was given only in secret revelations to the one disciple they had all agreed to despise: Judas Iscariot, the betrayer.

Judas alone, according to this hitherto lost view, knew the truth about Jesus. Jesus did not come from the creator of this world and was certainly not his son. He came from the realm of Barbelo to reveal the secret mysteries that could bring salvation. It was not his death that brought this salvation. His death simply released him from this evil material world. This world is a cesspool of pain, misery, and suffering, and our only hope of salvation is to forsake it. And some of us will do so. Some of us have a spark of the divine within, and when we die, we will burst forth from the prisons of our bodies and return to our heavenly home, the divine realm from which we descended and to which we will return, to live glorious and exalted lives forever.

IRENAEUS OF LYON
AND THE GOSPEL OF JUDAS

Gregor Wurst

Codex Tchacos, an ancient papyrus book from Egypt, originally contained at least four gnostic treatises, written in the Sahidic dialect of Coptic, an ancient language of Egypt. First in order is a badly preserved copy of the Letter of Peter to Philip, a text already known from the famous discovery at Nag Hammadi, Egypt, in 1945. The second is a much better preserved copy of a treatise named "James," which parallels the so-called First Revelation of James, also found within the Nag Hammadi library. The third is the Gospel of Judas, published here for the first time in an English translation. Finally, only parts of the opening pages survive of the fourth tractate, which has provisionally been called the Book of Allogenes by the editorial board of the codex. The Coptic language used in the codex is not the original language of these four texts. It is generally assumed that they were translated from Greek originals, as with all the Nag Hammadi texts. In the case of the Gospel of Judas, its name is found in ancient Christian literature, and this essay investigates a possible link between these ancient references and the newly discovered text. As a consequence, that will help us date the Greek original of the Gospel of Judas.

Early Witnesses: Irenaeus and Pseudo-Tertullian

The existence of a gospel of Judas is first attested by the late second-century bishop Irenaeus of Lyon, who mentions it in his famous treatise *Detection and Overthrow of the False Knowledge,* commonly entitled *Against Heresies.* Although it was originally written in Greek about 180, we possess this treatise only in a fourth-century Latin translation, while fragments of the Greek original survive through citations by later Christian writers addressing the problem of heresy. In appendices to his treatment of the "gnostics" and "other" gnostic believers, called "Ophites" ("Snake People") in later Christian tradition, Irenaeus turns to what he sees to be further subgroupings of these gnostics. He summarizes some of their teachings as follows:

> And others say that Cain was from the superior realm of absolute power, and confess that Esau, Korah, the Sodomites, and all such persons are of the same people as themselves: for this reason they have been hated by their maker, although none of them has suffered harm. For Wisdom [Sophia] snatched up out of them whatever belonged to her. And Judas the betrayer was thoroughly acquainted with these things, they say; and he alone was acquainted with the truth as no others were, and so accomplished the mystery of the betrayal. By him all things, both earthly and heavenly, were thrown into dissolution. And they bring forth a fabricated work to this effect, which they entitle the Gospel of Judas.

According to Irenaeus, this group of gnostics argues for a reevaluation of the Jewish and orthodox Christian ideas of divine salvation. Characters from the Jewish Scriptures such as Esau, Korah, and the Sodomites—regarded by the orthodox tradition as immoral and as rebels against the will of God—are considered here as the servants of the only true God, the "superior absolute power." This power, represented by the gnostic figure of Sophia, is not to be identified with the creator god of the Judeo-Christian tradition who is called here "their maker."

Even the most malicious figure in the New Testament, Judas Iscariot, the disciple who betrayed Jesus and delivered him to the authorities, is included in this reevaluation. He is regarded by these people as the only disciple—"of all the apostles," according to a Greek citation of this passage by the fifth-century writer Theodoret of Chyrrus—having the knowledge about "these things." Consequently, his deed is presented as a "mystery" leading to the dissolution of all earthly and heavenly things, that is, of all the works of the "maker" or ruler of this world.

From the beginning of the third century on, this group of gnostics was called "Cainites" ("followers of Cain") by Christian writers such as Clement of Alexandria. But most of these later Christian writers are simply dependent on Irenaeus's account. Only the third-century anonymous Latin treatise *Against All Heresies,* falsely ascribed to the early Christian writer Tertullian, and the account of the fourth-century Greek heresiologist (heresy hunter) Epiphanius of Salamis offer supplemental and more detailed information about the alternate view of Judas's act of betrayal within this circle—presumably going back to a lost heresiological treatise of Hippolytus of Rome. In chapter 2 of his treatise, Pseudo-Tertullian characterizes the teachings of the Cainites:

> Moreover, there has broken out another heresy, which is called that of the Cainites. And the reason is, that they magnify Cain as if he had been conceived of some potent virtue which operated in him; for Abel had been procreated after being conceived of an inferior virtue, and accordingly had been found inferior. They who assert this likewise defend the traitor Judas, telling us that he is admirable and great, because of the advantages he is vaunted to have conferred on humanity; for some of them think that thanksgiving is to be rendered to Judas on this account: Judas, they say, observing that Christ wished to subvert the truth, betrayed him, in order that there might be no possibility of truth's being subverted. And others thus dispute against them, and say: Because the powers of this world were unwilling that Christ should suffer, lest through his death salvation should be prepared for mankind, he, consulting for the salvation of humanity, betrayed Christ, in order that there might be no possibility at all of the salvation being impeded, which was being impeded through the virtues which were opposing Christ's passion; and thus, through the passion of Christ, there might be no possibility of the salvation of humanity being retarded.

According to this text, the Cainites held two interpretations of the act of Judas. On the one hand, they are said to hold the opinion that Jesus was prevented from "subverting the truth" by the betrayal, a view that remains very obscure for us and may be regarded as a typical distortion of an orthodox Christian writer who regarded this portrayal of Judas's deed as blasphemous. According to the other interpretation, Christ has been delivered to his death in order to enable salvation for humanity, which the "powers of this world"—that is, the inferior forces of the demiurge—were willing to impede. This statement is similar to what Irenaeus says about the "mystery of the betrayal" leading to the dissolution of the works of the inferior powers. But it is important to note that Pseudo-Tertullian does not mention the Gospel of Judas at all. His discussion is limited to what he believes to be the teachings of the Cainites. So that poses the question of whether we should regard the Gospel of Judas, mentioned by Irenaeus, as a Cainite work containing this kind of reevaluation of salvation or not. If so, the identification of Irenaeus's Gospel of Judas with the text within Codex Tchacos will be difficult, because in the newly discovered text there is no mention of Cain or the other antiheroes from the Jewish Scriptures mentioned by Irenaeus. As a result, we would have to assume the existence of more than one Gospel of Judas circulating within gnostic communities in antiquity.

HISTORICAL CONTENT
OF IRENAEUS'S ACCOUNT

Careful analysis of the account of Irenaeus shows that he does not count the Gospel of Judas among the writings originating among these "other" gnostics. He certainly knew of writings composed within that circle, as he states in the next sentence following the above citation: "I have also made a collection of their writings." But regarding the Gospel of Judas he states only that these people "bring forth" or "adduce" a "fabricated work" of that title in support of their view. This assertion implies merely that his opponents referred to a Gospel of Judas to uphold their view of the betrayer as someone endowed with special knowledge and destined to play an important role within their view of divine salvation; it does not necessarily imply that the gospel contained in addition their entire view of salvation. If this is correct, it is very uncertain that Irenaeus really knew the text of the gospel his opponents are alluding to. On the contrary, unlike the Cainite writings Irenaeus personally collected, he seemed to know the Gospel of Judas only from hearsay. For that reason we cannot be sure for which part of their teachings exactly these gnostics quoted the Gospel of Judas in support, with the exception of what they called the "mystery of the betrayal."

What can be deduced from the account of Irenaeus with certainty is that the Cainites read a Gospel of Judas and that they referred to it in support of their understanding of the act of the betrayal as a mystery. This implies that Judas was portrayed in that gospel as the disciple of Jesus "acquainted with the truth as no others were" and that the act of the betrayal must have been interpreted, in terms of a gnostic view of history of salvation, as part of the "dissolution of all earthly and heavenly things."

Comparison of the Coptic Gospel of Judas with Irenaeus's Account

These two thoughts run throughout the new Coptic Gospel of Judas. From the beginning, Judas Iscariot is portrayed as a disciple having a special knowledge about Jesus' true identity. He appears for the first time on page 35, where he is presented as the only disciple who is able to allow his inner, spiritual personality to come to expression before Jesus. In the same scene, Judas confesses to knowing who Jesus really is and where he comes from: "You are from the immortal realm of Barbelo," he says, "and I am not worthy to utter the name of the one who send you." And because Jesus knows that Judas is also reflecting upon "other exalted things," he exhorts him to part from the disciples and regards him as the only one worthy to be introduced into the "mysteries of the kingdom" (Gospel of Judas 35, 45).

Later on, Judas is set apart by Jesus for "that generation," that is, for the offspring of Seth, the true gnostics, and because of that he will become exalted over the other disciples (46). To Judas alone Jesus discloses the knowledge of the "great and boundless realm, whose extent no generation of angels has seen, [in which] there is [a] great invisible [Spirit], which no eye of an angel has ever seen, no thought of the heart has ever comprehended, and it was never called by any name" (47). What follows is the narration of the entire cosmological myth, ending with the creation of humanity by inferior gods (52–53).

All of this is in perfect accordance with the assertion of Irenaeus that the Judas of his Gospel of Judas is really "acquainted with the truth" as no other disciple of Jesus is. Our new Coptic text presents him in fact as the one to whom "everything has been told" (57). At the end, Judas *is* the perfect gnostic, worthy to be in a sense "transfigured" by ascending into a luminous cloud where he will receive his vision of the divine.

With regard to the place of Judas and his betrayal in the history of salvation, our new Coptic text is unfortunately not as clear. This is mainly due to extensive damage of the papyrus on the upper parts of the last pages. On pages 55–57 we can decipher some kind of prophecy from the mouth of Jesus about Judas's act, but several of the most important statements are broken away. The text reads as follows:

> But you will exceed all of them. For you will sacrifice the man that clothes me. Already your horn has been raised, your wrath has been kindled, your star has shown brightly, and your heart has [become strong]. Truly […] your last […] become [—*about two and a half lines missing*—], since he will be destroyed. And then the image of the great generation of Adam will be exalted, for prior to heaven, earth, and the angels, that generation, which is from the eternal realms, exists. Look, you have been told everything. (56–57)

This is clearly prophetic language. Jesus teaches Judas that he will have to play his part in the history of salvation, as he did earlier in the text when he announced that Judas would be replaced be someone else and would be cursed by the other disciples (36, 46). Judas's task is to sacrifice the body of Jesus. For what reason is not preserved, but we may guess that by this sacrifice the inner spirit of Jesus will be liberated. But this cannot be the whole story, because after a gap of about six lines, the text states that someone (or something) "will be destroyed" and that the "image of the great generation of Adam" will be exalted. What will be destroyed is made clear by Jesus on page 55: It is the "error of the stars," which are wandering about with their "five combatants," that "will be destroyed along with their creatures." So not only this world ("their creatures") will be destroyed, but also the heavenly powers that guide this world (the "stars" and the "combatants"). At the end, the "great generation of Adam," that is, the generation before Seth, will be saved. All this is also included in the word of Jesus that Judas "has been told everything."

It is important to notice that our newly discovered text mentions the destruction of heavenly (the "stars" and "combatants") and earthly realities ("their creatures") in the context of the act of the betrayal of Judas. Even if substantial parts of the text of our new gospel are lost in this passage, we can find here a close parallel to the statement of Irenaeus that by the act of Judas "all things, both earthly and heavenly, were thrown into dissolution."

Given the fact that the Gospel of Judas Irenaeus is discussing is certainly not a work written within the group of Irenaeus's opponents, given furthermore that he does not seem to have personal knowledge of it, but is only reporting what he knows from hearsay, a link between the new Coptic text from Codex Tchacos with the Gospel of Judas known from Irenaeus's account seems to be justified. We have seen that in the Coptic text Judas is presented as the only disciple of Jesus endowed with perfect knowledge, and we also find in the text points that can be paralleled with Irenaeus's statement that "all things, both earthly and heavenly, were thrown into dissolution." On this basis, and because we have no evidence to suppose that more than one Gospel of Judas circulated in antiquity, we can be confident in saying that the Gospel of Judas mentioned by Irenaeus is identical with the newly discovered Coptic Gospel of Judas. Consequently, we can assign a date prior to which the gospel had already been written in its original Greek: The Gospel of Judas had been written before 180, when Irenaeus noted that some of his opponents had mentioned it in support of their teachings.

The next question is *how long* before this date the Gospel of Judas was composed. This is very difficult to say, because we neither know its author nor have any detailed historical information about the Christian sect in which it originated. But one fact that can be stated with certainty is that the Gospel of Judas refers to the book of Acts from the New Testament. On page 36, Jesus says to Judas: "For someone else will replace you, in order that the twelve [disciples] may again come to completion with their god"—a clear allusion to the selection of Matthias to replace Judas in the circle of the twelve disciples (Acts 1:15–26). Since the book of Acts is generally dated about 90-100 by scholars of the New Testament, the Gospel of Judas must be placed in the second century. As a consequence, we cannot find here any more accurate historical information about Judas Iscariot than we find in the canonical gospels.

DATE OF CODEX TCHACOS

Since we do not have the original Greek text of the Gospel of Judas, we have to try to determine the date of the copy of its Coptic translation contained in Codex Tchacos. Since the codex was not found by archaeologists during a scientific excavation—in which case its date could be determined with a high degree of certainty—we can only apply the traditional method of comparing its design and the form of writing with other datable papyrus codices, such as those preserved within the Nag Hammadi library. This indicates a date in the first half of the fourth century, but dating manuscripts by this method is a delicate task and the degree of uncertainty remains high. A carbon-14 analysis executed by A. J. Timothy Jull from the University of Arizona dated the codex to around the last quarter of the third century (give or take a few decades). This dating may be confirmed by the investigation of the papyrus scraps (called cartonnage) used in the binding, or spine, of the codex, since such scraps—for example, tax receipts or other legal documents—normally are dated. But these papyrus scraps still have to be restored.

Conclusion

If this identification of the Gospel of Judas found in Codex Tchacos with the gospel Irenaeus mentioned is convincing, it will be an important step in the study of ancient gnosticism. Most of the Coptic texts from the Nag Hammadi library are extremely difficult to date. Even in the case of the Secret Book of John, a text attested in different versions in four Coptic manuscripts and by a comment of Irenaeus, ranking the priority of this or that version is far from being settled. But if the Gospel of Judas published here is the one in Irenaeus, we would have for first time the chance to trace back the history of Sethian gnosticism to before the time of Irenaeus.

In the case of this gospel, we have no reason to assume a complex history of editing, because it does not show the marks of subsequent reworking. This is not to say that textual alterations were not made while it was written. But there is no sign that extra parts, such as the revelation of the cosmology (Gospel of Judas 47–53), were written in as later additions. This kind of literary criticism would obviously destroy the original text.

The important result of this is that, if this text is identified as a Coptic translation of the Greek original mentioned by Irenaeus, then this version of Sethian cosmology also predates 180. So, this new text may possibly supply proven historical evidence that Sethian gnosticism is a movement prior to Irenaeus. This would be a significant gain in our knowledge of early Christianity.

Judas and the
Gnostic Connection

Marvin Meyer

I renaeus of Lyon, in *Against Heresies,* states that advocates of Cain, the wicked brother of Abel, composed the Gospel of Judas. Known as Cainites, this sect was accused by Irenaeus and other heresiologists of being champions of some of the most notorious characters in biblical literature, including Cain, Esau, Korah, the people of Sodom—and Judas Iscariot. Apart from these accusations, however, there is no historical evidence that any group of people within early Christianity called themselves Cainites; that name seems to be a nickname invented by heresy hunters. Nor is there any reference to Cain in the extant pages of the Gospel of

Judas, though theoretically his name could be lurking in a lacuna.

Yet there may be an element of truth in what Irenaeus has to say. Cain is mentioned in texts from the Nag Hammadi library, including the Secret Book of John, the Nature of the Rulers, and the Holy Book of the Great Invisible Spirit (the Egyptian Gospel), and two of these, the Secret Book and the Holy Book, contain passages on Cain as an angelic ruler of the world that, apart from the explicit reference to Cain, closely parallel a portion of the Gospel of Judas (51–52). The Holy Book also praises the people of Sodom and Gomorrah for their insight, as rebels with a cause. In other respects, too, these texts that mention Cain are related to the Gospel of Judas.

In his *Panarion,* or "Medicine Chest," with an antidote for every heretical malady, another heresiologist, Epiphanius of Salamis, associates the advocates of Cain and writers of the Gospel of Judas with people he terms "so-called gnostics," *gnōstikoi,* a Greek word that means "knowers" or "people of knowledge." Although some scholars criticize the word *gnostic* as too broad of an umbrella term, covering many different types of beliefs, Irenaeus says that in fact certain religious groups referred to themselves as "gnostics." The knowledge claimed by these people is not worldly knowledge but mystical knowledge, knowledge of God and self and the relationship between God and self. In the Gospel of Judas, the word *gnōsis* is used twice (50, 54), and in the second instance the text mentions "knowledge to be [given] to Adam and those with him, so that the kings of chaos and the underworld might not lord it over them." This passage suggests that the knowledge coming to Adam and the descendants of Adam—the human race—offers protection and salvation from the powers of this world. As Bart Ehrman also points out in his essay, the Gospel of Judas and Jesus himself in this gospel thus proclaim salvation through knowledge, the self-knowledge of the divine light within.

The gnostics discussed by Irenaeus and others constitute a major school of mystical religious thought in antiquity and late antiquity. Today scholars commonly refer to the students of that school of thought as Sethian gnostics, and when we refer to gnostics in a more general way, we extend the use of that term to include those groups that are related to Sethian gnostics. The Nag Hammadi texts noted for their interest in Cain all are part of this Sethian gnostic school, with the Secret Book of John regarded as the classic text of Sethian thought. The Gospel of Judas is also included in this school, representing an early form of Christian Sethian thought.

The central confession of Judas Iscariot, the hero of the Gospel of Judas, places the gospel in the Sethian gnostic tradition. In the gospel, the other disciples misunderstand who Jesus is and claim him to be the son of their God, the God of this world, but Judas declares to Jesus:

> I know who you are and where you have come from. You are from the immortal realm of Barbelo. And I am not worthy to utter the name of the one who has sent you. (Gospel of Judas 35)

The phrase "the immortal realm [or aeon] of Barbelo" is a familiar phrase in Sethian texts. It indicates the exalted realm of the divine beyond this world, and it is associated with the divine figure Barbelo, who is a prominent character in Sethian writings, where she often assumes the role of our Mother in heaven.

The origin of Barbelo and her name remains obscure, but it may come from the ineffable four-letter name of God, YHWH or Yahweh—Jehovah in Elizabethan English—used in the Jewish Scriptures and within Judaism. The Hebrew word for "four," *arba,* may designate the holy name, and the name of Barbelo may derive from Hebrew for an expression like "God (compare *El*) in (*b-*) four (*arb(a)*)," that is, God as known through the ineffable name.

In the extant Gospel of Judas, the figure of Barbelo isn't expanded into a character in a mythic drama, as in other Sethian texts, and the precise identity of Barbelo remains uncertain. It isn't even clear that she is the divine Mother; nor is Barbelo mentioned in the account, later in the gospel (47), of the appearance of Autogenes the Self-Generated. Barbelo is mentioned only once in the Gospel of Judas, by Judas himself, and his affirmation of the ineffability of the divine name may recall the holiness of the divine name within the Jewish heritage. Judas confesses that Jesus is from the divine, and he does not take the name of the divine in vain.

Whatever the precise meaning of the name is, Barbelo becomes the divine originator of light and life and the source—often the Mother—of the divine Child in Sethian texts. If Jesus, as Judas confesses in the Gospel of Judas, is from the immortal realm of Barbelo, he too is a divine being from the realm above.

John Turner, a scholar who has specialized in the study of the Sethians, gives a convenient summary of the most significant cosmological figures of Sethian thought:

> Many Sethian treatises locate at the summit of the hierarchy a supreme triad of Father, Mother, and Child. The members of this triad are the Invisible Spirit, Barbelo, and the divine Autogenes. The Invisible Spirit seems to tran-

scend even the realm of being itself, which properly begins with Barbelo as his projected self-reflection. The Child is self-generated (*autogenēs*) from Barbelo either spontaneously or from a spark of the Father's light, and is responsible for the ordering of the remainder of the transcendent realm, which is structured around the Four Luminaries and their associated aeons. The realm of becoming below this usually originates from Sophia's attempt to instantiate her own contemplation of the Invisible Spirit all by herself and without its permission; in many accounts, this act produces her misshapen offspring the Archon as the maker of the phenomenal world.

Sethian texts frequently portray the world we inhabit with features drawn from their interpretation of Adam and Eve, which are used to tell a remarkable and revolutionary story. The creator of the world, according to Sethians, is actually a megalomaniacal demiurge, but human beings are exalted above the creator and his powers by virtue of the spark of divinity within them. If people come to know their true divine selves, they will be able to escape the clutches of the powers of this world and realize the peace of enlightenment.

In the Gospel of Judas, Jesus reveals to Judas what he and readers of the text need to know in order to achieve a proper understanding of who Jesus is and what life in the world and beyond entails. At the same time, the Sethian perspective of the Gospel of Judas is representative of early Sethian thought, and the Sethian themes of the gospel are not fully developed. The Gospel of Judas, I propose, may thus provide a glimpse of Sethian Christians in the process of developing their version of the good news of Jesus.

THE GREAT ONE, BARBELO, AND AUTOGENES THE SELF-GENERATED

The Gospel of Judas proclaims its cosmological message about the divine in a typically Sethian way. Barbelo is mentioned, as are the Father and Autogenes the Self-Generated. The Father or Parent of All is identified as a "great invisible [Spirit]" in one passage within the extant pages of the Gospel of Judas (47), as he is in many Sethian texts, and he is also described in a number of additional places throughout the Gospel of Judas as great and invisible (47) and Spirit (49)— and as "the Great One" (53). It appears to be inappropriate to speak of the Great One as "God" in the Gospel of Judas; that term seems to be reserved for lower powers of the universe and for the creator of this world, for "all those called 'God'" (48). In the Gospel of Judas, the Great One seems to transcend the finite term *God*. The same theological point is made in the Secret Book of John:

> The One is a sovereign that has nothing over it. It is God and Parent, Father of All, the invisible one that is over All, that is incorruptible, that is pure light at which no eye can gaze. The One is the invisible Spirit. We should not think of it as a God or like a God. For it is greater than a God, because it has nothing over it and no lord above it. It does not [exist] within anything inferior [to it, since everything] exists within it, [for it established] itself. (Nag Hammadi Codex II, 2–3)

The transcendence of the Great One is emphasized in the Gospel of Judas. When Jesus reveals the secrets of the universe to Judas, he uses phrases to depict the divine that recall the language of 1 Corinthians 2:9, Gospel of Thomas 17, the Prayer of the Apostle Paul in the Nag Hammadi library, and other texts. Jesus says:

> [Come], that I may teach you about [secrets] no person [has] ever seen. For there exists a great and boundless realm, whose extent no generation of angels has seen, [in which] there is [a] great invisible [Spirit],

which no eye of an angel has ever seen,
no thought of the heart has ever comprehended,
and it was never called by any name. (47)

Other Sethian texts, especially the Secret Book of John and Allogenes the Stranger, present fuller descriptions of the transcendence of the divine. In the Secret Book of John, the revealer says:

> *The One is*
> *illimitable, since there is nothing before it to limit it,*
> *unfathomable, since there is nothing before it to fathom it,*
> *immeasurable, since there was nothing before it to measure it,*
> *invisible, since nothing has seen it,*
> *eternal, since it exists eternally,*
> *unutterable, since nothing could comprehend it to utter it,*
> *unnamable, since there is nothing before it to give it a name.*
>
> *The One is the immeasurable light, pure, holy, immaculate.*
> *It is unutterable, and is perfect in incorruptibility.*
> *Not that it is just perfection, or blessedness, or divinity: it is much greater.*
>
> *The One is not corporeal and it is not incorporeal.*

> *The One is not large and it is not small.*
> *It is impossible to say,*
> *How much is it?*
> *What {kind is it}?*
> *For no one can understand it. (II:3)*

This description reminds us again of the words of Judas to Jesus near the beginning of the Gospel of Judas: "I am not worthy to utter the name of the one who has sent you" (35).

Autogenes the Self-Generated is discussed in Gospel of Judas 47–50 when Jesus reveals the glorious manner in which the divine extends itself and comes to full expression. The Great One, the great invisible Spirit, transcends all aspects of this world of mortality here below, so some manifestation of the divine must bring about the creation and salvation of the world. That manifestation is Autogenes the Self-Generated. Jesus states that from a luminous heavenly cloud, showing the brilliance of the divine, comes a divine voice calling for an angel, and from the cloud Autogenes the Self-Generated appears. *Autogenes* is a term commonly used in Sethian texts to characterize the offspring of Barbelo, and the term underscores the independence of the Child: The Child, as Autogenes, is a self-starter. The name Autogenes or "Self-Generated" works particularly well in the Gospel of Judas, where the Self-Generated simply emerges, by himself, from the heavenly cloud after the voice calls out.

Elsewhere in Sethian literature, the account of the appearance of the Child Autogenes can become more complicated, and in the longer version of the Secret Book of John, the appearance of the Child is portrayed in such a way as to suggest an act of spiritual intercourse between the transcendent Father and Barbelo the Mother:

> The Father gazed into Barbelo, with the pure light surrounding the invisible Spirit, and his radiance. Barbelo conceived from him, and he produced a spark of light similar to the blessed light but not as great. This was the only Child of the Mother-Father that had come forth, the only offspring, the only Child of the Father, the pure light. The invisible virgin Spirit rejoiced over the light that was produced, that came forth from the first power of the Spirit's Forethought, who is Barbelo. (II:6)

In the Gospel of Judas, Jesus goes on to recount how four other angels, or messengers, called "luminaries," come into being through the Self-Generated, and they serve as attendants for the Self-Generated (47). In other Sethian stories, the Four Luminaries are assigned names: Harmozel, Oroiael, Daveithai, and Eleleth. Increasing numbers of angels and aeons—heavenly beings—come into existence, "myriads without number," according to the Gospel of Judas, as the brilliance of the divine is expressed. Eventually the expansion of the divine extends to the aeons, luminaries, heavens, and firmaments of the universe, and their numbers correspond to features of the world, especially units of time. There are twelve aeons, like the number of months in a year or signs in the zodiac. There are seventy-two heavens and luminaries, like the traditional number of nations in the world according to Jewish lore. There are three hundred sixty firmaments, like the number of days in the solar year (less the five intercalary days). The number twenty-four is also used, as the number of hours in a day (Gospel of Judas 49–50).

This section of the Gospel of Judas is so closely paralleled by passages in the text Eugnostos the Blessed and a related text, the Wisdom of Jesus Christ, that I believe some sort of textual relationship is possible. The author of Eugnostos the Blessed describes the production of aeons and other powers in two relevant passages:

> The twelve powers I have discussed came together with each other, and each produced <six> males and <six> females, for a total of 72 powers. Each of the 72 in turn produced five spiritual powers, bringing the number to 360 powers. They are united in will. In this way

immortal humanity came to symbolize our realm. The first one to conceive, the son of immortal humanity, functions as a symbol of time. The [savior] symbolizes [the year]. The twelve powers are symbols of the twelve months. The 360 powers who derive from the savior stand for the 360 days of the year. And the angels who came from them and who are without number stand for the hours and minutes. (Nag Hammadi Codex III: 83–84)

Some of these, in dwellings and chariots, were in ineffable glory and could not be sent into any creature, and they produced for themselves hosts of angels, myriads without number, to serve and glorify them, as well as virgin spirits and ineffable lights. They are free of sickness and weakness. There is only will, and it comes to expression at once. (III:88–89)

In the Gospel of Judas, these theological reflections, intricate and complex as they are, disclose a sophisticated way of thinking about the divine. In the beginning, it is said, there is the infinite, unnamable, ineffable deity—if we may even call the Great One a "deity" or, for that matter, use any finite word whatsoever to describe the One. The Great One expands through aeons and countless entities to a fullness of divine glory that shines down toward our world below. Were it not for a tragic mistake in the divine realm, a lapse of wisdom, all would have remained glorious. But a lapse did occur.

Corruptible Sophia and the Creator

According to Sethian texts, the fall from grace at the beginning of time was a divine event of cosmic proportions. In the Bible, Genesis 3 narrates the story of Adam and Eve yielding to the will of the serpent and eating from the tree of the knowledge of good and evil, against the will of God. Sethian texts speak of divine Wisdom, personified as Sophia, who shares traits with Eve and falls into an error that would have grave consequences. The surviving portion of the Gospel of Judas doesn't include the story of Sophia and the fall of Sophia. There is only a single reference to Sophia in a fragmentary part of the text, where, with little explanation, she is called "corruptible Sophia." Following a gap, there is a reference to "the hand that has created mortal people," which may link Sophia to the god who creates this world.

In the Secret Book of John, the account of the fall of Wisdom is presented in some detail:

> Now Sophia, who is the Wisdom of Insight and
> who constitutes an aeon, conceived of a thought

from herself, with the conception of the Invisible Spirit and Foreknowledge. She wanted to bring forth something like herself, without the consent of the Spirit, who had not given approval, without her partner and without his consideration. The male did not give approval. She did not find her partner, and she considered this without the Spirit's consent and without the knowledge of her partner. Nonetheless, she gave birth. And because of the invincible power within her, her thought was not an idle thought. Something came out of her that was imperfect and different in appearance from her, for she had produced it without her partner. It did not resemble its mother, and was misshapen. (II:9–10)

In the Letter of Peter to Philip, the revealer in the text provides a further crucial detail of the fall of Mother Sophia. In the Codex Tchacos version of the letter, the revealer says:

To begin with, [concerning] the deficiency of the aeons, what is deficient is disobedience. The Mother, showing poor judgment, came to expression without the command of the Great One. He is the one who wished, from the beginning, to set up aeons. But when she [spoke], the Arrogant One appeared. A body part from within her was left behind, and the Arrogant One grabbed it, and deficiency came to be. This, then, is the deficiency of the aeons. (3–4)

The word *deficiency* also occurs in Gospel of Judas 39. The deficiency, or diminution in the divine light, comes from a bad conception, according to the Secret Book of John, and from disobedience and poor judgment, according to the Letter of Peter to Philip. The Mother of the Letter of Peter to Philip could be either Sophia or Eve, and considering the connection between Sophia and Eve in gnostic literature, the ambiguity may be deliberate. As the story of Sophia unfolds in the literature, part of the divine spirit passes from Sophia to her child, the creator of this world, who eventually blows it—right into humanity (Genesis 2:7). Thus, Sophia's loss means that human beings have the light of the divine within.

This is the larger story of "corruptible Sophia" in the Gospel of Judas. All that is deficient in the world of the divine and the world below stems from the lapse of Wisdom, and when the light within people becomes one with the divine again, then Sophia is restored and the fullness of the divine is realized. Something of that bliss may be experienced now, gnostic texts suggest, but the final experience of divine wholeness occurs when people leave their mortal bodies. In the Gospel of Judas, Jesus says that when people of the generation of Seth—gnostics—pass away, their physical bodies die but their souls remain alive and return, liberated, to their heavenly home (43). At death, all that belongs to the body and is at home in this world of mortality is to be relinquished. The mortal bodies of people of knowledge are to be surrendered, Jesus says to Judas, "so that their souls [go] up to the eternal realms above" (44).

In some gnostic traditions, particularly Valentinian traditions, two figures of Wisdom are mentioned, higher Wisdom and lower Wisdom, probably in an effort to deal with the delicate issue of how to affirm the supreme goodness of the divine and still acknowledge the reality of evil in a flawed world. This issue, the question of theodicy or the problem of evil, remains one of the most difficult and significant of issues in theological discussions to the present day. What is evil, and where does it come from? Is God somehow involved in evil? In the Valentinian Gospel of Philip, higher Wisdom is called Sophia or Echamoth, lower Wisdom Echmoth, "the Wisdom of death" (Nag Hammadi Codex II, 60), and the higher Wisdom of God is shielded from the evil of this mortal world. Similarly, perhaps, the Holy Book of the Great Invisible Spirit also makes mention of "Sophia of matter" (Nag Hammadi Codex III, 57).

How the reference to "corruptible Sophia" in the Gospel of Judas relates to the more fully developed ways of construing Wisdom in gnostic texts remains uncertain. What is clear is that she is "corruptible."

The offspring of Sophia and the product of her mistake, described as a misshapen child in the Secret Book of John and dubbed "the Arrogant One" in the Letter of Peter to Philip, is the chief ruler and the creator of this world, well known from Sethian texts. In the Gospel of Judas and other gnostic traditions, the creator of this world is not a kind and gentle figure. As creator and demiurge, he is responsible for keeping the divine light of Sophia imprisoned within mortal bodies. In Gospel of Judas 51, the creator is named Nebro and Yaldabaoth, and another, Saklas, collaborates with him. Forms of all three names are known from other Sethian sources. *Yaldabaoth* most likely means "child of chaos," and *Saklas* means "fool." The name Nebroel or Nebruel occurs in the Holy Book of the Great Invisible Spirit and Manichaean sources; in the Gospel of Judas, the name Nebro is spelled without the honorific suffix *-el* (meaning "God" in Hebrew). In the Holy Book, Nebruel seems to be a demoness who has sex with Sakla and gives birth to twelve aeons (III:57).

Jesus in the Gospel of Judas uses graphic language to tell Judas what the creator of this world looks like, and he is not a handsome demiurge. Jesus says, "Look, from the cloud there appeared an [angel] whose face flashed with fire and whose appearance was defiled with blood" (51). When his face flashes with fire, he looks like Yaldabaoth in the Secret Book of John (II:10), and when he is defiled with blood, he looks like Sophia of matter in the Holy Book of the Great Invisible Spirit (III:56–57).

The creator and his lackeys, according to the Gospel of Judas, create this world below with rulers, angels, and powers all around. The institution of the bureaucracy of angelic powers is portrayed in a passage that is slightly damaged:

> The twelve rulers spoke with the twelve angels: "Let each of you [...] and let them [...] generation [—*one line lost*—] angels":
>
> The first is [S]eth, who is called Christ.
> The [second] is Harmathoth, who is [...].
> The [third] is Galila.
> The fourth is Yobel.
> The fifth [is] Adonaios.
>
> These are the five who ruled over the underworld, and first of all over chaos. (51–52)

Parallels to this passage are found in the Secret Book of John (II:10–11) and the Holy Book of the Great

Invisible Spirit (III:58), and these parallels depict the same sort of bureaucracy of rulers of the world as the Gospel of Judas, albeit in a more full-blown way. The Holy Book reads:

> Through the will of the Self-Generated, [Sakla] the great angel said, "There shall be ... seven in number...."
>
> He said to the [great angels], "Go, [each] of you reign over your own [world]." And each [of these] twelve [angels] left.
>
> [The first] angel is Athoth, whom [the great] generations of people call ... ,
> the second is Harmas, [the eye of fire],
> the third [is Galila],
> the fourth is Yobel,
> [the fifth is] Adonaios, who is [called] Sabaoth,
> the sixth [is Cain, whom] the [great generations of] people call the sun,
> the [seventh is Abel],
> the eighth, Akiressina,
> the [ninth, Youbel],
> the tenth is Harmoupiael,
> the eleventh is Archir-Adonin,
> the twelfth [is Belias].
> These are set over Hades [and chaos].

The Secret Book of John states that seven are placed over the seven spheres of heaven (for the sun, moon,

Mercury, Venus, Mars, Jupiter, and Saturn) and five over the depths of the abyss.

The bureaucrats of this world are in place in the Gospel of Judas, and this abyss of a world—the cosmos, "perdition" according to Gospel of Judas 50—is ready to be occupied. All it needs is a family of tenants.

SETH AND THE CREATION OF ADAM AND EVE

The figure of Seth, the third son of Adam and Eve, is a significant figure in the Gospel of Judas. The Gospel of Judas lists Seth (also called Christ) as an angelic ruler of the world, and it refers to "the generation of Seth" (also called "the great generation," "that generation," and "the generation with no ruler over it") and the parents of Seth, Adam and Eve, as well as Adamas, described as heavenly Adam in a cloud of light. What does all of this mean? In the Bible, the first family is highly dysfunctional: The parents get into trouble with God and are evicted from their garden home, and the first two boys, Cain and Abel, both come to bad ends. Seth, Genesis 4–5 reports, is born to Adam and Eve as another son, "another seed," produced in the image of Adam just as Adam was produced in the image of God. He is the one who carries on the family of Adam. Further, Genesis reports that Seth himself has a son, Enoch, and at that time people begin to call upon the Lord Yahweh with his holy name.

Apparently because Seth is "another seed," he inherits the epithet Allogenes, which means "one of another kind" or "stranger" in Greek. There is a Sethian text in Nag Hammadi Codex XI, which I already mentioned, entitled Allogenes, or Allogenes the Stranger, and Porphyry the Neoplatonic author cites a "revelation of Allogenes" that may be this very text from the Nag Hammadi library (*Life of Plotinus* 16). Moreover, Epiphanius refers to multiple books of Allogenes (or Allogeneis, in the plural; *Panarion* 39.5.1).

A fragment of the book identified as the fourth and last tractate of Codex Tchacos, immediately after the Gospel of Judas, has been given the provisional title Book of Allogenes on account of the main character within the text. We might wonder whether this text could possibly be one of the other books of Allogenes. In the last tractate of Codex Tchacos, as in other Christian Sethian texts, Allogenes takes on the role of Jesus. In the text, Jesus is Seth the Stranger incarnated as the Christian savior, and in the person of Allogenes he faces temptations by Satan and experiences transfiguration in a luminous cloud—just as Judas is transfigured in a luminous cloud in the Gospel of Judas (57–58).

In good Platonic fashion, in keeping with the Platonic interests of the Sethian tradition, Adam in the Gospel of Judas is both an ideal figure of humanity above as well as an earthly figure below. Adam, called Adamas (probably a pun on the Greek word *adamas,* "steel-like," "unbreakable"), "was in the first luminous cloud that no angel has ever seen among all those called 'God'" (48). A little later reference is made to "the incorruptible [generation] of Seth" (49). While in the Gospel of Judas Seth is not explicitly placed with Adamas in the divine realms, as in other Sethian texts, Jesus states near the end of the text that "prior to heaven, earth, and the angels, that generation [the generation of Seth], which is from the eternal realms, exists" (57). Such a statement of the exalted place of origin of the generation of Seth may imply that Seth himself is also assumed to be an exalted figure in the divine realms in the Gospel of Judas.

The Secret Book of John gives a more detailed account. According to the Secret Book, heavenly Adamas resides in the first aeon with the first luminary Harmozel, in a manner reminiscent of the heavenly home of Adamas in the Gospel of Judas, and Seth resides in the second aeon with the second luminary Oroiael (II:9). The seed of Seth also dwells in heaven, as in the Gospel of Judas; according to the Secret Book of John, the seed of Seth is in the third aeon with the third luminary Daveithai. In the Secret Book of John, heavenly Adam is named Pigeradamas (or Geradamas)—"Adam the stranger," "holy Adam," or "old Adam."

The fact that heavenly Adamas is said in the Gospel of Judas to be in the first luminous cloud means that he dwells in the glory of the divine, close to the Great One. This close connection between Adamas, ideal humanity, and the Great One confirms what was suggested by scholar Hans-Martin Schenke. Schenke saw a close link between the supreme deity in gnostic thought and the archetypal human, so that, in different ways and with different patterns, transcendent humanity comes to be associated with the transcendent One. This connection between God and Man in Sethian texts is exemplified in the primal revelation of the divine in Sethian texts, where the divine voice rings out from above, "Humanity exists, and the child of humanity" (or, "Man exists, and the son of man"; Secret Book of John II:14).

The story of the creation of earthly Adam and Eve and their children in the Gospel of Judas, concise as it is, is told with biblical and Platonic themes: "Then Saklas said to his angels, 'Let us create a human being after the likeness and after the image'" (52). This follows the account of Genesis and interprets it in Platonic and gnostic terms. Genesis 1:26 states that the creator makes humanity after the image and likeness of the divine, and in Sethian traditions this is interpreted to mean that earthly Adam is patterned after the ideal image of heavenly Adamas. This gnostic idea of a ruler of earth creating human beings here below after the image and in the form of the transcendent human in the heavenly realm above is similar to the Platonic belief that the demiurge creates the world on the basis of forms and ideas from the realm of ideas.

Other gnostic texts, including Sethian texts, offer similar reflections upon Genesis 1:26. The Letter of Peter to Philip has Jesus describe the creative work of the Arrogant One as the production of "an image instead of an [image], a form instead of a form" (4). In the Secret Book of John, the account is much more developed, and it distinguishes between creation in the image of the divine and creation in the likeness of the archons and authorities of the world:

> A voice called from the exalted heavenly realm, "Humanity exists, and the child of humanity." The first ruler, Yaldabaoth, heard the voice and thought it had come from his mother. He did not realize its source. The holy perfect Mother-Father, the complete Forethought, the image of the invisible One, being the Father of All, through whom everything came into being, the

first human—this is the one who showed them and appeared in human shape. The entire realm of the first ruler quaked, and the foundations of the abyss shook. The bottomside of the waters above the material world was lit up by this image that had appeared. When all the authorities and the first ruler stared at this appearance, they saw the whole bottomside as it was lit up. And through the light they saw the shape of the image in the water. Yaldabaoth said to the authorities with him, "Come, let us create a human being after the image of God and with a likeness to ourselves, so that this human image may give us light." They created through their respective powers, according to the features that were given. Each of the authorities contributed a psychical feature corresponding to the figure of the image they had seen. They created a being like the perfect first human, and said, "Let us call it Adam, that its name may give us power of light." (II:14–15)

One of the distinctive features of the Gospel of Judas is its emphasis upon astronomical and astrological concerns, particularly the role of the stars and planets in human life, and this emphasis likewise seems to be based upon Platonic themes. Other Sethian texts also comment on the ways in which the powers of the sky rule over people, but the Gospel of Judas says that a person is given a soul and is guided by a star. In the Gospel of Judas, Jesus tells Judas that people have souls, but only the people of the generation of Seth have souls that are immortal:

> The souls of every human generation will die.
> When these people, however, have completed
> the time of the kingdom and the spirit leaves
> them, their bodies will die but their souls will
> be alive, and they will be taken up. (43)

Here and elsewhere in the text, the spirit of a person may be contrasted with the soul. The spirit may be the breath of life, while the soul may be the inner person who comes from the divine and returns to the divine. The same contrast helps to explain what Jesus means when he teaches Judas, in Gospel of Judas 53, that although ordinary people have spirits in them for a period of time, people of the generation of Seth have both spirits and souls from the Great One. Jesus also reflects upon the stars, and in Gospel of Judas 42, Jesus remarks to Judas and the other disciples, "Each of you has his own star."

The interest in souls and stars recalls Plato's statements on souls, stars, and the creation of the world. In the *Timaeus*, Plato has Timaeus cite a statement by the creator of the world, and then Timaeus comments on how souls are assigned to stars:

Thus the creator spoke, and once more into the cup in which he had previously mingled the soul of the universe he poured the remains of the elements and mingled them in much the same manner; they were not, however, pure as before, but diluted to the second and third degree. And having made it, he divided the whole mixture into souls equal in number to the stars, and assigned each soul to a star; and having there placed them as in a chariot, he showed them the nature of the universe, and declared to them the laws of destiny, according to which their first birth would be one and the same for all—no one should suffer a disadvantage at his hands; they were to be sown in the instruments of time severally adapted to them, and to come forth the most religious of animals; and as human nature was of two kinds, the superior race would here after be called humanity.... The person who lived well during his appointed time was to return and dwell in his native star, and there he would have a blessed and congenial existence. (41d–42b; ed. Benjamin Jowett, slightly revised)

The native star of Judas is blessed, Jesus tells him near the end of the Gospel of Judas. Judas may be destined for grief, as he is warned throughout the text, and he will become the thirteenth one, the outcast from the circle of the twelve disciples, cursed by others and replaced in the circle of the twelve by another (Gospel of Judas 35–36; Acts 1:15–26). So, Jesus calls Judas the "thirteenth spirit" (44), literally the "thirteenth demon," using the term used by Plato for the guiding spirit of Socrates and others. In spite of all the difficulty and opposition faced by Judas, Jesus promises that the future will bring him blessing and joy, and as Bart Ehrman notes in his essay, thirteen turns out to be a lucky number for Judas. Jesus tells Judas to look up and recognize that among all the stars above, his star leads the way (57).

By the middle of the third century, Sethian texts that incorporated these sorts of Platonic themes and numerous concepts from Middle Platonism and Neoplatonism were in circulation, and some of them were discussed and critiqued by the Neoplatonic philosopher Plotinus and the students in his philosophical school in Rome. These Platonizing Sethian texts read in Rome may include tractates from the Nag Hammadi library, such as Allogenes the Stranger, as we have seen. One of the complaints of the Platonists against the gnostics and their texts was that they were too hard on the demiurge—Nebro, Yaldabaoth, Saklas—and they portrayed him in too negative a fashion. It is true that Sethian texts have little good to say about the creator of this world, and to that extent Sethians may have been out of step with other Platonists. Nonetheless, it is evident that Sethian texts, including the Gospel of Judas, embraced themes derived from Plato, and in their own way they worked them into their understanding of the divine and the universe.

The Gospel of Judas as a Christian Sethian Text

As I have tried to show in this essay, the Gospel of Judas appears to be an early Christian Sethian gospel with teachings of Jesus presented to Judas Iscariot, to announce a way of salvation and enlightenment based upon knowledge of self and the divine. The message of the Gospel of Judas is that, just as Jesus is a spiritual being who has come from above and will return to glory, so also the true followers of Jesus are people of soul, whose being and destiny are with the divine. Already those who know themselves can live in the strength of the inner person, the "perfect human" mentioned by Jesus in his comments to the disciples (35). At the end of their mortal lives, people who belong to that great generation of Seth will abandon everything of this mortal world, in order to free the inner person and liberate the soul.

In the Gospel of Judas, that kind of sacrifice is what Jesus asks of his dear friend and most insightful disciple: He asks Judas to help liberate him from his mortal body by handing him over to the authorities. Others also sacrifice, Jesus tells Judas, but what Judas will do is the best gift of all. Jesus says to Judas, "But you will exceed all of them. For you will sacrifice the man that clothes me" (56). Judas could do no less for his friend and soul mate, and he betrays him. That is the good news of the Gospel of Judas.

The gospel's teachings are those of Jesus the Christian savior, and the story recounts the betrayal of Jesus, yet the major instruction given by Jesus about cosmology and the secret things of the universe (Gospel of Judas 47–53) contains very little that could be considered specifically Christian. This cosmological account is based on innovative Jewish concepts and interpretations of Jewish Scripture and is influenced by Platonic ideas; the only indisputably Christian element in the entire account is the brisk reference to "[S]eth, who is called Christ" (Gospel of Judas 52). The cosmological account thus seems to have had its origin in an earlier Jewish Sethian context, and it has been taken over and lightly Christianized as the teaching of Jesus. In other words, Jewish Sethian teaching is transformed into Christian Sethian teaching in the Gospel of Judas.

Such a transformation is also evident elsewhere in gnostic literature. The Secret Book of John is another Sethian text that seems to have been composed as a Jewish gnostic document and lightly Christianized into the teaching and revelation of Jesus. Similarly, Eugnostos the Blessed is a Jewish gnostic text, in the form of a letter, that has been edited and expanded into the teachings of Jesus in dialogue with his disciples, in the Wisdom of Jesus Christ.

Jesus, then, is understood to be the teacher and revealer of knowledge in the Gospel of Judas. He is from the divine and will return to the divine, and he gives instruction to Judas and members of the generation of Seth. In other Sethian Christian texts, Jesus takes on a similar role, and commonly he is associated with Barbelo, Autogenes the Self-Generated, and Seth. In the Secret Book of John, Christ is identified with the Self-Generated and becomes the son of divine Barbelo (II:6–7). In the Holy Book of the Great Invisible Spirit, Seth is clothed with "the living Jesus," and Jesus becomes the incarnation of Seth. In the Book of Allogenes from Codex Tchacos, Jesus is presented as Allogenes the Stranger, a form of Seth. In the Three Forms of First Thought, the *Logos* or Word, with links to Seth, announces that it has put on Jesus and has carried him from the cursed wood (Nag Hammadi

Codex XIII, 50). Jesus in the Gospel of Judas is also associated with Barbelo, but the nature of their relationship is unclear; and how Jesus relates to Autogenes the Self-Generated, if at all, is unknown. And the only explicit connection between Jesus and Seth in the Gospel of Judas is in the list of the angelic figures who rule over chaos and the underworld.

Questions remain about the associations and relationships of Jesus according to the Gospel of Judas, but not about his proclamation. Jesus proclaims a mystical message of hope and freedom, articulated in Sethian gnostic terms. He leaves Judas and the readers of the gospel with a word of enlightenment and liberation, and he urges Judas to look to the stars. As Jesus says to Judas in Gospel of Judas 57, "Lift up your eyes and look at the cloud and the light within it and the stars surrounding it. The star that leads the way is your star."

ENDNOTES

The Gospel of Judas

PAGE 44...{*—about five lines missing—*}...A new fragment was placed on the top of pages 57 and 58 of Codex Tchacos as this book went to press. The new readings are in the present translation, but the fragment is not visible in the photograph of the Gospel of Judas on page vi.

Gregor Wurst

PAGE 121...*written in the Sahidic dialect of Coptic...*Coptic is the language of Egyptian Christianity and the last phase of the Egyptian language, that is, the language of the pharaohs, written with the letters of the Greek alphabet plus some additional letters derived form Demotic, a cursive form of writing the hieroglyphic script. Sahidic is one of the two main dialects of the Coptic language.

PAGE 122...*the Book of Allogenes...*Photographs of the main parts of the first four pages of this text, together with photographs of the last two pages of the Gospel of Judas, have circulated during recent years among scholars. This led to the impression that the four pages also form part of the gospel. However, the analysis of the papyrus, to be published in the upcoming critical edition, has proven that these pages are the opening part of a fourth tractate whose badly preserved title may be restored as "The B[ook of Allogenes]."

PAGE 122...*treatment of the "gnostics"...*On the significance of the terms *gnosis* and *gnostics*, cf. the essay of Marvin Meyer in this volume.

PAGE 123 *And others say that Cain...which they entitle the Gospel of Judas.* English translation by Bentley Layton, *The Gnostic Scriptures: A New Translation with Annotations and Introductions* (Garden City, NY: Doubleday, 1987), 181 (slightly adapted).

PAGE 123...*Esau, Korah, and the Sodomites*...For Esau, cf. Genesis 25:19–34, 27:32–33; for Korah, Genesis 36:5 and Numbers 16–17; and for the Sodomites, Genesis 18–19.

PAGE 124...*this group of gnostics was called "Cainites"*...Cf. Birger A. Pearson, *Gnosticism, Judaism, and Egyptian Christianity,* Studies in Antiquity and Christianity (Minneapolis: Fortress, 1990), 95–107. Pearson argues that a particular Cainite sect of gnostics never existed in antiquity. According to him, "The Cainite system of *gnosis*, delineated as such by the heresiologists, is nothing but a figment of their imagination, an artificial construct."

PAGE 124...*dependent on Irenaeus's account.* For the most complete survey of ancient Christian sources relating to the Cainites and to the Gospel of Judas, cf. the article by Clemens Scholten, "Kainiten," in *Reallexikon für Antike und Christentum* (Stuttgart: Anton Hiersemann, 2001), 19:972–73; cf. also Wilhelm Schneemelcher, ed., *New Testament Apocrypha* (English translation edited by Robert McLachlan Wilson; rev. ed.; Cambridge, England: James Clarke; Louisville, KY: Westminster/John Knox, 1991–92), 1:386–87.

PAGE 125 *Moreover, there has broken...humanity being retarded.* Translation from Alexander Roberts and James Donaldson, eds., *Ante-Nicene Fathers: Translations of the Writings of the Fathers down to A.D. 325* (Buffalo, NY: Christian Literature Publishing Company, 1885–96; reprint, Peabody, MA: Hendrickson, 1994), 3:651 (slightly adapted).

PAGE 127...*more than one Gospel of Judas*...As it is the case with the famous Gospel of Thomas, also known mainly through a Coptic translation in Nag Hammadi Codex II, *2.* In addition to that, another Gospel of Thomas is extant, which belongs to the so-called infancy gospels and whose content is completely different from the Nag Hammadi text.

PAGE 127...*among these "other" gnostics.* As rightly pointed out by Clemens Scholten ("Kainiten," 975). Scholten even asked whether the last sentence of Irenaeus's account presupposes the existence of a written Gospel of Judas at all.

PAGE 127...*"bring forth" or "adduce"*...The Latin word *adferunt,* used by the translator of Irenaeus here, can be translated "they bring forth," "they adduce," or even "they produce," so that interpretation depends heavily on the translation adopted.

PAGE 128...*all earthly and heavenly things."* This interpretation is held also by Hans-Josef Klauck; see his *Judas: Ein Jünger des Herrn,* Quaestiones Disputatae 111 (Freiburg: Herder, 1987), 19–21.

PAGE 129...*the offspring of Seth*...On "that generation" and the offspring of Seth, see the essay by Marvin Meyer.

PAGE 131...*someone (or something)*...It is not clear to whom or what this pronominal subject refers. In the Coptic text, it refers to a male antecedent.

PAGE 124...*far from being settled.* This is due to the fact that no version of the

Secret Book of John transmitted by the different Coptic witnesses can be identified as the source of Irenaeus in *Against Heresies* 1.29. In fact, the Secret Book of John has undergone substantial editing within its history of transmission, so that every theory identifying this or that textual form as the original depends on substantial literary criticism and thus remains conjectural; cf. John D. Turner, *Sethian Gnosticism and the Platonic Tradition*, Bibliothèque copte de Nag Hammadi, Section "Études" 6 (Sainte Foy, Québec: Presses de l'Université Laval; Louvain: Peeters, 2001), 136–41.

MARVIN MEYER

PAGE 137...*Irenaeus and other heresiologists*...On the heresiologists and the Gospel of Judas, see the essay by Gregor Wurst. Here and below, the references are to Irenaeus *Against Heresies* 1.31.1 and Epiphanius *Panarion* 38.1–3. For a translation of Irenaeus and other heresiological texts against the so-called Cainites, cf. Werner Foerster, ed., *Gnosis: A Selection of Gnostic Texts,* (Oxford: Clarendon Press, 1972, 1974), 1:41–43; and (Irenaeus only) Bentley Layton, *The Gnostic Scriptures: A New Translation with Annotations and Introductions* (Garden City, NY: Doubleday, 1987), 181.

PAGE 138...*texts from the Nag Hammadi library*...On the Nag Hammadi library, cf. Jean-Pierre Mahé and Paul-Hubert Poirier, eds., *Écrits gnostiques,* Bibliothèque de la Pléiade (Paris: Gallimard, 2007 [in press]); Marvin Meyer, *The Gnostic Discoveries: The Impact of the Nag Hammadi Library* (San Francisco: HarperSanFrancisco, 2005); Marvin Meyer, ed., *The Nag Hammadi Scriptures: The International Edition* (San Francisco: HarperSanFrancisco, 2006 [in press]); James M. Robinson, ed., *The Nag Hammadi Library in English*, 3rd ed. (San Francisco: HarperSanFrancisco, 1988); Hans-Martin Schenke, Hans-Gebhard Bethge, and Ursula Ulrike Kaiser, eds., *Nag Hammadi Deutsch*, 2 vols., Die Griechischen Christlichen Schriftsteller der ersten Jahrhunderte, Neue Folge 8, 12 (Berlin: Walter de Gruyter, 2001, 2003).

PAGE 138...*"knowers" or "people of knowledge."* On the use of the word *gnostic* and related terms, and the nature of gnostic thought, cf. Layton, *Gnostic Scriptures;* Bentley Layton, "Prolegomena to the Study of Ancient Gnosticism," in L. Michael White and O. Larry Yarbrough, eds., *The Social World of the First Christians: Essays in Honor of Wayne A. Meeks* (Minneapolis: Fortress, 1995), 334–50; Antti Marjanen, ed., *Was There a Gnostic Religion?;* Publications of the Finnish Exegetical Society 87 (Göttingen: Vandenhoeck & Ruprecht, 2005); Meyer, *Gnostic Discoveries,* 38–43; Marvin Meyer, *The Gnostic Gospels of Jesus: The Definitive Collection of Mystical Gospels and Secret Books about Jesus of Nazareth* (San Francisco: HarperSanFrancisco, 2005), x–xiii; Marvin Meyer, "Gnosticism, Gnostics, and *The Gnostic Bible*," in Willis Barnstone and Marvin Meyer, eds., *The Gnostic Bible* (Boston: Shambhala, 2003), 1–19; Birger A. Pearson, *Gnosticism and Christianity in Roman and Coptic Egypt,* Studies in Antiquity and Christianity (New York: Clark International, 2004), 201–23; Kurt Rudolph, *Gnosis: The Nature and History of Gnosticism,* English translation ed. Robert McLachlan Wilson (San Francisco: HarperSanFrancisco, 1987).

PAGE 138...*covering many different types of beliefs*...Cf. Karen L. King, *What Is Gnosticism?* (Cambridge, MA: Belknap Press/Harvard University Press, 2003); Michael A. Williams, *Rethinking "Gnosticism": An Argument for Dismantling a Dubious Category* (Princeton, NJ: Princeton University Press, 1996).

PAGE 139...*groups that are related to Sethian gnostics.* Cf. Hans-Martin Schenke, "The Phenomenon and Significance of Sethian Gnosticism," in Bentley Layton, ed., *The Rediscovery of Gnosticism: Proceedings of the International Conference on Gnosticism at Yale, New Haven, Connecticut, March 28–31, 1978,* Studies in the History of Religions (Supplements to Numen) 41 (Leiden: E. J. Brill, 1980–81), 2:588–616; Hans-Martin Schenke, "Das sethianische System nach Nag-Hammadi-Handschriften," in Peter Nagel, ed., *Studia Coptica* (Berlin: Akademie Verlag, 1974), 165–72; John D. Turner, "Sethian Gnosticism: A Literary History," in Charles W. Hedrick and Robert Hodgson Jr., eds., *Nag Hammadi, Gnosticism, and Early Christianity* (Peabody, MA: Hendrickson, 1986), 55–86; John D. Turner, *Sethian Gnosticism and the Platonic Tradition,* Bibliothèque copte de Nag Hammadi, Section "Études" 6 (Sainte Foy, Québec: Presses de l'Université Laval; Louvain: Peeters, 2001); Michael A. Williams, "Sethianism," in Antti Marjanen and Petri Luomanen, eds., *A Companion to Second-Century "Heretics,"* Supplements to *Vigiliae Christianae* 76 (Leiden: E. J. Brill, 2005), 32–63.

PAGE 140 **The central confession of Judas Iscariot...** It is Peter who offers a confession of who Jesus is in the New Testament synoptic gospels; cf. Matthew 16:13–20; Mark 8:27–30; Luke 9:18–21. When Jesus asks his disciples who people say he is, Matthew has the disciples answer that some say Elijah and others Jeremiah or another prophet, and Peter says, "You are the Christ, the son of the living God"; Mark has Peter saying, "You are the Christ," Luke has "God's Christ." Cf. the profession of the disciples in Gospel of Judas 34. Thomas offers his statement about Jesus in Gospel of Thomas 13:

> Jesus said to his disciples, "Compare me to something and tell me what I am like." Simon Peter said to him, "You are like a just messenger." Matthew said to him, "You are like a wise philosopher." Thomas said to him, "Teacher, my mouth is utterly unable to say what you are like." Jesus said, "I am not your teacher. Because you have drunk, you have become intoxicated from the bubbling spring that I have tended." And he took him, and withdrew, and spoke three sayings to him. When Thomas came back to his friends, they asked him, "What did Jesus say to you?" Thomas said to them, "If I tell you one of the sayings he spoke to me, you will pick up rocks and stone me, and fire will come from the rocks and consume you."

PAGE 140...*God as known through the ineffable name.* Cf. W. W. Harvey, ed., *Irenaeus, Libros quinque adversus haereses* (Cambridge: Academy, 1857; reprint, Ridgewood, NJ: Gregg, 1965), 221–2.

PAGE 141-42 **Many Sethian treatises...maker of the phenomenal world.** Turner, *Sethian Gnosticism,* 85. The citation is slightly modified, in consultation with the author.

PAGE 144 **The One is a sovereign...(Nag Hammadi Codex II, 2–3).** The translations of Nag Hammadi texts throughout this essay are my own. Cf. Meyer, *Gnostic Gospels of Jesus;* Meyer, *Nag Hammadi Scriptures.*

PAGE 144...*and other texts.* Paul writes, in 1 Corinthians 2:9, "But as it is written, 'What no eye has seen and no ear has heard, and what has not arisen in the human heart, what God has prepared for those who love him.'" Gospel of Thomas 17 reads: "Jesus said, 'I shall give you what no eye has seen, what no ear has heard, what no hand has touched, what has not arisen in the human heart.'" The passage from the Prayer of the Apostle Paul is cited in the notes to the translation. Cf. also Michael E. Stone and John Strugnell, *The Books of Elijah: Parts 1–2,* Society of Biblical Literature Texts and Translations 18, Pseudepigrapha 8 (Missoula, MT: Scholars, 1979).

PAGE 145-46 *The one is...For no one can understand it.* Allogenes the Stranger includes a passage (Nag Hammadi Codex XI, 61–64) that closely parallels this section of the Secret Book of John.

PAGE 147 *The Father gazed...who is Barbelo.* In the shorter version of the Secret Book of John, it is said that Barbelo gazes into the Father, turns to him, and then gives birth to a spark of light (cf. Berlin Gnostic Codex 8502, 29–30; Nag Hammadi Codex III, 9).

PAGE 147...*Harmozel, Oroiael, Daveithai, and Eleleth.* The names and roles of the Four Luminaries are discussed in Turner, *Sethian Gnosticism.*

PAGE 148...*passages in the text Eugnostos the Blessed...*On Eugnostos the Blessed and the Wisdom of Jesus Christ, cf. Douglas M. Parrott, *Nag Hammadi Codices III,3–4 and V,1 with Papyrus Berolinensis 8502,3 and Oxyrhynchus Papyrus 1081: Eugnostos and the Sophia of Jesus Christ,* Nag Hammadi Studies 27, The Coptic Gnostic Library (Leiden: E. J. Brill, 1991).

PAGE 150...*the god who creates this world.* On wisdom, including personified Wisdom, in ancient and particularly Sethian thought, cf. Meyer, *Gnostic Discoveries,* 57–115.

PAGE 150-51 *Now Sophia...and was misshapen.* Sophia attempts to imitate the original procreative act of the Father. The account of Sophia giving birth by herself seems to reflect ancient gynecological theories about women's bodies and reproduction. In Greek mythology, the goddess Hera also imitates Zeus and brings forth a child by herself. According to one version of that story, the child is the monster Typhon (*Homeric Hymn to Pythian Apollo* 300–62). According to another, it is the lame deity Hephaistos, whom Hera evicts from Olympus and sends down to the world below (Hesiod *Theogony* 924–29). In the Secret Book of John, all the evils and misfortunes of this world derive from Sophia's blunder.

PAGE 151-52 *To begin with...deficiency of the aeons.* Here the Nag Hammadi version of the Letter of Peter to Philip reads as follows:

> To begin with, concerning [the deficiency] of the aeons, this is the deficiency. When the disobedience and foolishness of the Mother appeared, without the command of the majesty of the Father, she wanted to set up aeons. When she spoke, the arrogant one followed. But when she left behind a portion, the arrogant one grabbed it, and it became a deficiency. This is the deficiency of the aeons. (135)

PAGE 152 *The word* deficiency *also occurs...* The word *deficiency* is šōōt in the Coptic text of the Gospel of Judas. This term and similar words function as technical terms in Sethian and other texts for the loss of divine light due to the transgression of the Mother.

PAGE 152...*light of the divine within.* The Secret Book of John has the following colorful account (quoted here more fully than in the notes to the translation) of how the divine tricks Yaldabaoth, the creator of this world, into blowing divine light and spirit into humanity:

> When the Mother wanted to take back the power she had relin-
> quished to the first ruler, she prayed to the most merciful
> Mother-Father of All. With a sacred command the Mother-Father
> sent five luminaries down upon the place of the angels of the first
> ruler. They advised him so that they might recover the mother's
> power. They said to Yaldabaoth, "Breathe some of your spirit into
> the face of Adam, and the body will arise." He breathed his spir-
> it into Adam. The spirit is the power of his mother, but he did
> not realize this, because he lives in ignorance. The Mother's
> power went out of Yaldabaoth and into the psychical body that
> had been made to be like the one who is from the beginning. The
> body moved, and became powerful. And it was enlightened. At
> once the rest of the powers became jealous. Although Adam came
> into being through all of them, and they gave their power to this
> human, Adam was more intelligent than the creators and the first
> ruler. When they realized that Adam was enlightened, and could
> think more clearly than they, and was stripped of evil, they took
> and threw Adam into the lowest part of the whole material realm.
> (II:19–20)

PAGE 153...*higher Wisdom is called Sophia or Echamoth...* Here the Gospel of Philip reads, "There is Echamoth and there is Echmoth. Echamoth is simply Wisdom, but Echmoth is the Wisdom of death—that is, the Wisdom that knows death, that is called little Wisdom." Elsewhere (cf. the First Revelation of James, the Book of Baruch, and the heresiologists), lower Wisdom is named Achamoth, and she may be considered the daughter of higher Wisdom, Sophia. The names Echamoth and Achamoth both derive from the Hebrew word for wisdom, *Hokhmah;* Echmoth means "like death" in Hebrew and Aramaic *('ekh-moth).* Cf. Layton, *Gnostic Scriptures,* 336.

PAGE 153...*"Sophia of matter"...* Here the Holy Book of the Great Invisible Spirit reads, "A cloud [named] Sophia of matter appeared." This passage is cited more fully in the notes to the translation.

PAGE 154...*are known from other Sethian sources.* Other texts, such as the Secret Book of John, the Nature of the Rulers, and On the Origin of the World, also refer to the creator of this world as Samael, a name that means "blind god" in Aramaic.

PAGE 154...*and gives birth to twelve aeons.* On Nebro, Hebrew Nimrod, and the Greek Nebrod of the Septuagint, cf. the notes to the translation.

PAGE 155 *When his face flashes with fire...* On these descriptions, cf. the passages cited in the notes to the translation.

PAGE 155 *...The fifth {is} Adonaios...* The name Adonaios derives from the Hebrew *Adonai,* "my Lord," supplied with the Greek masculine ending *-os.* The figure Adonaios plays a significant role in gnostic literature. Cf. Secret Book of John; On the Origin of the World; Holy Book of the Great Invisible Spirit; Second Discourse of Great Seth; Book of Baruch.

PAGE 157 *The figure of Seth...* On the role of Seth in Sethian and other texts, cf. Birger A. Pearson, "The Figure of Seth in Gnostic Literature," in Layton, *Rediscovery of Gnosticism,* 2:471–504; Pearson, *Gnosticism and Christianity,* 268–82; Birger A. Pearson, *Gnosticism, Judaism, and Egyptian Christianity,* Studies in Antiquity and Christianity (Minneapolis: Fortress, 1990), 52–83; Gedaliahu A. G. Stroumsa, *Another Seed: Studies in Gnostic Mythology* (Leiden: E. J. Brill, 1984); Turner, *Sethian Gnosticism.*

PAGE 159 *...according to the Secret Book of John...* Here the Secret Book of John reads:

> From the Foreknowledge of the perfect Mind, through the expressed will of the invisible Spirit and the will of the Self-Generated, came the perfect human, the first revelation, the truth. The virgin Spirit named the human Pigeradamas, and appointed Pigeradamas to the first eternal realm with the great Self-Generated, the anointed, by the first luminary, Harmozel. Its powers dwell with it. The invisible one gave Pigeradamas an invincible power of mind. Pigeradamas spoke and glorified and praised the Invisible Spirit by saying, "Because of you everything has come into being, and to you everything will return. I shall praise and glorify you, the Self-Generated, the eternal realms, the three, Father, Mother, Child, perfect power." Pigeradamas appointed his son Seth to the second eternal realm, before the second luminary, Oroiael. In the third eternal realm were stationed the offspring of Seth, with the third luminary, Daveithai. The souls of the saints were stationed there. In the fourth eternal realm were stationed the souls of those who were ignorant of the Fullness. They did not repent immediately, but held out for a while and repented later. They came to be with the fourth luminary, Eleleth. These are creatures that glorify the Invisible Spirit.

PAGE 160 *..."Adam the stranger," "holy Adam," or "old Adam."* On the possible etymologies of Pigeradamas or Geradamas, cf. Meyer, *Gnostic Gospels of Jesus,* 312–13.

PAGE 160 *This close connection between Adamas...* Hans-Martin Schenke, *Der Gott "Mensch" in der Gnosis: Eine religionsgeschichtliche Beitrag zur Diskussion über die paulinische Anschauung von der Kirche als Leib Christi* (Göttingen: Vandenhoeck & Ruprecht, 1962).

PAGE 161 *..."an image instead of an [image]"...* On the expression "an image instead of an [image]," cf. Gospel of Thomas 22:

Jesus said to them, "When you make the two into one, and when you make the inner like the outer and the outer like the inner, and the upper like the lower, and when you make male and female into a single one, so that the male will not be male nor the female be female, when you make eyes in place of an eye, a hand in place of a hand, a foot in place of a foot, an image in place of an image, then you will enter [the kingdom]."

PAGE 163-64 *Thus the creator spoke...blessed and congenial existence.* Benjamin Jowett, ed., *Timaeus* (New York: Liberal Arts Press, 1949); also available at *Internet Classics Archive*, http://classics.mit.edu/Plato/timaeus.html.

PAGE 165...*Sethian texts that incorporated these sorts of Platonic themes...*On Platonizing Sethian texts, cf. Turner, *Sethian Gnosticism*.

SELECTED BIBLIOGRAPHY

Barnstone, Willis, and Marvin Meyer, eds. *The Gnostic Bible*. Boston: Shambhala, 2003.

Bauer, Walter. *Orthodoxy and Heresy in Earliest Christianity*. Philadelphia: Westminster, 1971.

Bethge, Hans-Gebhard, Stephen Emmel, Karen L. King, and Imke Schletterer, eds. *For the Children, Perfect Instruction: Studies in Honor of Hans-Martin Schenke on the Occasion of the Berliner Arbeitskreis für koptisch-gnostische Schriften's Thirtieth Year*. Nag Hammadi and Manichaean Studies 54. Leiden: E. J. Brill, 2002.

Brown, Raymond. *The Death of the Messiah*. 2 vols. New York: Doubleday, 1994.

Brox, Norbert. *Offenbarung, Gnosis und gnostischer Mythos bei Irenäus von Lyon*. Salzburger patristische Studien 1. Salzburg: Pustet, 1966.

Crum, Walter E. *A Coptic Dictionary*. Oxford: Clarendon Press, 1939.

Culianu, Ioan. *The Tree of Gnosis: Gnostic Mythology from Early Christianity to Modern Nihilism*. San Francisco: HarperSanFrancisco, 1992.

Doresse, Jean. *The Secret Books of the Egyptian Gnostics: An Introduction to the Gnostic Coptic Manuscripts Discovered at Chenoboskion*. New York: Viking, 1960; reprint, New York: MJF Books, 1997.

Ehrman, Bart D. *After the New Testament: A Reader in Early Christianity*. New York: Oxford University Press, 1998.

———. *Jesus: Apocalyptic Prophet of the New Millennium*. New York: Oxford University Press, 1999.

———. *Lost Christianities: The Battles for Scripture and the Faiths We Never Knew*. New York: Oxford University Press, 2003.

———. *Lost Scriptures: Books That Did Not Make It into the New Testament*. New York: Oxford University Press, 2003.

Foerster, Werner, ed. *Gnosis: A Selection of Texts*. 2 vols. Oxford: Clarendon Press, 1972, 1974.

Jonas, Hans. *The Gnostic Religion: The Message of the Alien God and the Beginnings of Christianity*. 2nd ed. Boston: Beacon, 1963.

Kasser, Rodolphe. *Compléments au dictionaire copte de Crum*. Bibliothèque des études coptes 7. Cairo: Institut français d'archéologie orientale, 1964.

―――. *L'Évangile selon Thomas: Présentation et commentaire théologique*. Neuchâtel: Delachaux & Niestlé, 1961.

―――. *Papyrus Bodmer VI: Livre des Proverbes*. Corpus Scriptorum Christianorum Orientalium 194–95, Scriptores Coptici 27–28. Louvain: Corpus Scriptorum Christianorum Orientalium, 1960.

Kasser, Rodolphe, in collaboration with Colin Austin. *Papyrus Bodmer XXV–XXVI: Ménandre, La Samienne; Le Bouclier*. Cologny, Switzerland: Bibliotheca Bodmeriana, 1969.

Kasser, Rodolphe, in collaboration with Sébastien Favre, Denis Weidmann, et al. *Kellia: Topographie*. Recherches suisses d'archéologie copte 2. Geneva: Géorg, 1972.

Kasser, Rodolphe, Michel Malinine, Henri-Charles Puech, Gilles Quispel, and Jan Zandee, eds. *Tractatus Tripartitus: Pars I, Pars II, Pars III*. 2 vols. Bern: Francke, 1973, 1975.

Kasser, Rodolphe, in collaboration with Victor Martin. *Papyrus Bodmer XIV–XV: Évangile de Luc, chap. 3–24; Évangile de Jean, chap. 1–15*. Cologny, Switzerland: Bibliotheca Bodmeriana, 1961.

King, Karen L. *The Gospel of Mary of Magdala: Jesus and the First Woman Apostle*. Santa Rosa, CA: Polebridge Press, 2003.

―――. *What Is Gnosticism?* Cambridge, MA: Belknap Press/Harvard University Press, 2003.

Klassen, William. *Judas: Betrayer or Friend of Jesus?* Minneapolis: Fortress, 1996.

Klauck, Hans-Josef. *Judas: Ein Jünger des Herrn*. Quaestiones Disputatae 111. Freiburg: Herder, 1987.

Klijn, A. F. J. *Seth in Jewish, Christian, and Gnostic Literature*. Leiden: E. J. Brill, 1977.

Krause, Martin, and Pahor Labib, eds. *Die drei Versionen des Apokryphon des Johannes im Koptischen Museum zu Alt-Kairo*. Abhandlungen des Deutschen Archäologischen Instituts Kairo, Koptische Reihe. Wiesbaden: Harrassowitz, 1962.

―――. *Gnostische und hermetische Schriften aus Codex II und VI*. Abhandlungen des Deutschen Archäologischen Instituts Kairo, Koptische Reihe. Glückstadt: J. J. Augustin, 1971.

Layton, Bentley. *A Coptic Grammar with Chrestomathy and Glossary: Sahidic Dialect*. Porta Linguarum Orientalium, n.s. 20. Wiesbaden: Harrassowitz, 2000.

―――. *The Gnostic Scriptures: A New Translation with Annotations and Introductions*. Garden City, NY: Doubleday, 1987.

Maccoby, Hyam. *Judas Iscariot and the Myth of Jewish Evil*. New York: Free Press, 1992.

Mahé, Jean-Pierre, and Paul-Hubert Poirier, eds. *Écrits gnostiques*. Bibliothèque de la Pléiade. Paris: Gallimard, 2007 [in press].

Markschies, Christoph. *Gnosis: An Introduction*. London: T. & T. Clark, 2003.

Meyer, Marvin. *The Gnostic Discoveries: The Impact of the Nag Hammadi Library*. San Francisco: HarperSanFrancisco, 2005.

―――. *The Gnostic Gospels of Jesus: The Definitive Collection of Mystical Gospels and Secret Books about Jesus of Nazareth*. San Francisco: HarperSanFrancisco, 2005.

―――. *The Gospel of Thomas: The Hidden Sayings of Jesus*. San Francisco: HarperSanFrancisco, 1992.

―――, ed. *The Nag Hammadi Scriptures: The International Edition*. San Francisco: HarperSanFrancisco, 2006 [in press].

Paffenroth, Kim. *Judas: Images of the Lost Disciple.* Louisville, KY: Westminster/John Knox, 2001.

Pagels, Elaine H. *Beyond Belief: The Secret Gospel of Thomas.* New York: Random House, 2003.

———. *The Gnostic Gospels.* New York: Random House, 1979.

Pearson, Birger A. *Gnosticism and Christianity in Roman and Coptic Egypt.* Studies in Antiquity and Christianity. New York: T. & T. Clark International, 2004.

———. *Gnosticism, Judaism, and Egyptian Christianity.* Studies in Antiquity and Christianity. Minneapolis: Fortress, 1990.

Puech, Henri-Charles, ed., *Histoire des religions: II, La formation des religions universelles et des religions du salut dans le monde méditerranéen et le Proche-Orient, les religions constituées en Occident et leurs contre-courants.* Encyclopédie de la Pléiade. Paris: Gallimard, 1973.

Robinson, James M., ed. *The Nag Hammadi Library in English.* 3rd ed. San Francisco: HarperSanFrancisco, 1988.

Rudolph, Kurt. *Gnosis: The Nature and History of Gnosticism.* English translation edited by Robert McLachlan Wilson. San Francisco: HarperSanFrancisco, 1987.

Schenke, Hans-Martin, Hans-Gebhard Bethge, and Ursula Ulrike Kaiser, eds. *Nag Hammadi Deutsch.* 2 vols. Die Griechischen Christlichen Schriftsteller der ersten Jahrhunderte, Neue Folge 8, 12. Berlin: Walter de Gruyter, 2001, 2003.

Schenke, Hans-Martin, and Rodolphe Kasser, eds. *Papyrus Michigan 3520 und 6868(a): Ecclesiastes, erster Johannesbrief und zweiter Petrusbrief im Fayumischen Dialekt.* Berlin: Walter de Gruyter, 2003.

Schneemelcher, Wilhelm, ed. *New Testament Apocrypha.* 2 vols. English translation edited by R. McL. Wilson. Rev. ed. Cambridge, England: James Clarke; Louisville, KY: Westminster/John Knox, 1991–92.

Scholer, David M. *Nag Hammadi Bibliography, 1948–1969.* Nag Hammadi Studies 1. Leiden: E. J. Brill, 1971.

———. *Nag Hammadi Bibliography, 1970–1994.* Nag Hammadi Studies 32. Leiden: E. J. Brill, 1997.

Sevrin, Jean-Marie. *Le dossier baptismal séthien: Études sur la sacramentaire gnostique.* Bibliothèque copte de Nag Hammadi, Section "Études" 2. Sainte Foy, Québec: Presses de l'Université Laval, 1986.

Stroumsa, Gedaliahu A. G. *Another Seed: Studies in Gnostic Mythology.* Leiden: E. J. Brill, 1984.

Turner, John D. *Sethian Gnosticism and the Platonic Tradition.* Bibliothèque copte de Nag Hammadi, Section "Études" 6. Sainte Foy, Québec: Presses de l'Université Laval; Louvain: Peeters, 2001.

Unger, Dominic J., ed. *St. Irenaeus of Lyons: Against the Heresies, Book 1.* Ancient Christian Writers 55. Westminster, MD: Newman, 1992.

Van Oort, Johannes, Otto Wermelinger, and Gregor Wurst, eds. *Augustine and Manichaeism in the Latin West: Proceedings of the Fribourg-Utrecht International Symposium of the International Association of Manichaean Studies.* Leiden: E. J. Brill, 2001.

Williams, Michael A. *Rethinking "Gnosticism": An Argument for Dismantling a Dubious Category.* Princeton, NJ: Princeton University Press, 1996.

Wurst, Gregor. *Das Bemafest der ägyptischen Manichäer.* Arbeiten zum spätantiken und koptischen Ägypten 8. Altenberge: Oros, 1995.

———. *The Manichaean Coptic Papyri in the Chester Beatty Library: Psalm Book, Part II, Fasc. 1: Die Bema-Psalmen.* Corpus Fontium Manichaeorum, Series Coptica 1, Liber Psalmorum Pars 2, Fasc. 1. Turnhout: Brepols, 1996.

PUBLISHER'S NOTE

When Zurich antiquities dealer Frieda Tchacos Nussberger acquired the ancient codex that included the Gospel of Judas in 2000, it had been for sale for nearly twenty years and carried from Egypt to Europe to the United States. Rodolphe Kasser, a Swiss expert in such Coptic texts, says he had never seen one in worse shape. "The manuscript was so brittle that it would crumble at the slightest touch." Alarmed by its deterioration, Tchacos turned it over to the Maecenas Foundation for Ancient Art, which will restore and translate the manuscript and ultimately give it to Cairo's Coptic Museum. The codex project, which combined archaeology, cutting-edge science, and a subject of cultural interest, was a natural for National Geographic. The Society enlisted the support of the Waitt Institute for Historic Discovery, a foundation created by Gateway founder Ted Waitt to support projects that improve mankind's knowledge through historical and scientific exploration. The Society and the Waitt Institute would work with the Maecenas Foundation to authenticate the document, continue the restoration process, and translate the contents of the codex. But first, conservator Florence Darbre, assisted by Coptic scholar Gregor Wurst, had to resurrect the tattered text.

Someone had rearranged the pages, and the top of the papyrus (with the page numbers) had broken away. A greater challenge: Almost a thousand fragments lay scattered like crumbs. Darbre picked up the fragile pieces with tweezers and laid them between sheets of glass. With the help of a computer, she and Wurst were able to reassemble more than 80 percent of the text in five painstaking years. Kasser and other scholars translated the twenty-six page document, a detailed account of long-hidden gnostic beliefs. Scholars of early Christianity say it is the most dramatic textual discovery in decades. Says Kasser, "This script comes back to light by a miracle."

In order to be certain of its age and authenticity, the National Geographic Society put the codex through the closest scrutiny possible without doing it harm. This included submitting minute samples of the papyrus to the most rigorous radiocarbon dating process available and consulting with leading Coptic scholars well versed in the fields of paleography and codicology.

In December 2004, the National Geographic Society hand-delivered the five minuscule samples to the University of Arizona's radiocarbon-dating Accelerated Mass Spectrometry (AMS) lab in Tucson, Arizona.

Four samples were papyrus pieces from the codex, while a fifth was a small section of leather book binding with papyrus attached. No portion of the text was damaged in this process.

In early January 2005, scientists at the AMS lab completed their radiocarbon-dating testing. While individual samples calibrated ages varied, the mean calendar age for the collection was between CE 220 and 340, with an error margin of +/- sixty years.

According to AMS Lab Director Dr. Tim Jull and research scientist Greg Hodgins, "the calibrated ages of the papyrus and leather samples are tightly clustered and place the age of the Codices within the Third or Fourth centuries A.D."

Since its discovery in the late 1940s, radiocarbon dating has been the gold standard for dating ancient objects and artifacts in fields ranging from archaeology to paleoclimatology. The development of accelerated mass spectrometry technology has enabled researchers to sample many tiny fragments of an artifact, as was done in the case of the codex.

The University of Arizona's AMS Lab is world-renowned for its work—including precision-dating the Dead Sea Scrolls, which enabled scholars to place the scrolls accurately within their correct historical context.

The content and linguistic style of the codex is further evidence of its authenticity, according to leading scholars who have studied it. These experts included Drs. Rodolphe Kasser, former professor of the University of Geneva, and a leading translator of the Nag Hammadi library; Marvin Meyer of Chapman University (Orange, CA); and Stephen Emmel, professor of Coptic studies at the University of Münster (Germany). All three were instrumental in the translation of this codex.

According to these scholars, the codex's theological concepts and its linguistic structure are very similar to concepts found in the Nag Hammadi library, a collection of mostly gnostic texts discovered in Egypt in the 1940s that also date to the early centuries of Christianity.

"This text coheres very well with known ideas of the second century of the common era. Even in its fragmentary form it is very interesting—it fits very well into the second century, nicely into a certain part of the second century," Dr. Meyer said.

Emmel concurs with Meyer's view that the content of the codex reflects a unique gnostic worldview prevalent in the second century. "[To fabricate such a document] you would have to reflect a world that is totally foreign to any world we know today. A world that is fifteen hundred years old ... That is very difficult for scholars even who spend their lives studying these things to understand, let alone to create for other people. It would take a real genius to produce an artifact like this and personally I don't think it possible," he said.

"I have no doubt whatsoever that this codex is a genuine artifact of late antique Egypt and that it contains evidence for genuine works of ancient Christian apocryphal literature," Emmel added.

In addition to reflecting a gnostic world view, the paleographic evidence also supports the codex's authenticity. Dr. Emmel—an expert in Coptic paleography—or handwriting, gave this assessment: "It is carefully written by someone who is a professional scribe. The kind of writing reminds me very much of the Nag Hammadi codices. It's not identical script with any of them. But it's a similar type of script."

"The question of whether or not someone in modern times could fake an object like this is for me a non-question—it's out of the question. One would not only have to have genuine material, papyrus, and not simply any papyrus, but ancient papyrus. One would also have to know how to imitate Coptic script from a very early period. The number of specialists in Coptic that know that in the world is very small. You would also have to compose a text in Coptic that is grammatically correct and convincing. The number of people who could do that is even smaller than the number who could read Coptic."

In a further effort to absolutely ensure the codex's authenticity, samples of the ink were sent to McCrone and Associates—a firm well known for its work in forensic ink analysis. This analysis again confirmed the document's authenticity.

Transmission electron microscopy (TEM) confirmed the presence of carbon black as a major constituent of the ink, and the binding medium is a gum—which is consistent with inks from the third and fourth centuries CE.

Using a method known as Raman spectroscopy, McCrone and Associates was further able to establish that the ink contained a metal-gallic ink component consistent with the iron gall inks used in the third century.

RODOLPHE KASSER, PH.D., a professor emeritus on the Faculty of Arts at the University of Geneva, is one of the world's leading Coptologists. He has organized the restoration and prepared the *editio princeps* of Codex Tchacos, containing the Gospel of Judas and three other Coptic Gnostic texts.

MARVIN MEYER, PH.D., Griset Professor of Bible and Christian Studies at Chapman University and Director of the Chapman University Albert Schweitzer Institute, is one of the foremost scholars on Gnosticism, the Nag Hammadi Library and texts about Jesus outside the New Testament.

GREGOR WURST, PH.D., is a professor of Ecclesiastical History and Patristics at the University of Augsburg, Germany.

BART D. EHRMAN, PH.D., is the James A. Gray Distinguished Professor and Chair of the Department of Religious Studies, University of North Carolina at Chapel Hill, and an expert on early Christianity.